FOOL'S GOLD?

FOOL'S

GOLD?

DISCERNING TRUTH IN AN AGE OF ERROR

JOHN MACARTHUR

GENERAL EDITOR

NATHAN BUSENITZ, SCOTT LANG, PHIL JOHNSON

ASSOCIATE EDITORS

CROSSWAY BOOKS

A MINISTRY OF
GOOD NEWS PUBLISHERS
WHEATON, ILLINOIS

Library of Congress Cataloging-in-Publication Data
Fool's gold? : discerning truth in an age of error / John MacArthur, general editor ; Nathan Busenitz, Scott Lang, Phil Johnson, associate editors.
    p. cm.
    Includes bibliographical references and index.
    ISBN 1-58134-726-X (tpb)
    1. Christian life—Biblical teaching. 2. Discernment (Christian theology). 3. Evangelicalism. I. MacArthur, John, 1939-   . II. Busenitz, Nathan. III. Lang, Scott, 1966-   . IV. Johnson, Phillip R., 1953-   .
BS680.C47F66   2005
230'.04624—dc22   2004030155

DP		15	14	13	12	11	10	09	08	07	06	05
15	14	13	12	11	10	9	8	7	6	5	4	3	2	1

*Dedicated to the faithful pastors and church leaders
who have partnered with us through the
Shepherds' Conference and Shepherds' Fellowship.*

May the Lord bless your ministry as you continue serving Him.

CONTENTS

PART FOUR
Pursuing Discernment in Your Daily Life

ABOUT THE
CONTRIBUTORS

Nathan Busenitz *is the director of the Shepherds' Fellowship (a non-denominational association of churches spearheaded by Grace Community Church) as well as an adjunct faculty member at The Master's College & Seminary. In addition, he is the managing editor of Pulpit, the online magazine of the Shepherds' Fellowship. Nathan graduated from The Master's Seminary in 2002. He and his wife, Bethany, have two children, Ashley and Isaac. Nathan is also the author of Living a Life of Hope (Barbour Books, 2003).*

Dan Dumas serves as executive pastor of Grace Community Church as well as pastor of the Cornerstone fellowship group (a ministry to young marrieds and families). He also oversees conferences and conference planning. Dan graduated from The Master's Seminary in 2001. Before coming to Grace Church, Dan served as college and singles pastor at the Westside Baptist Church in Jacksonville, Florida, and Cottage Hill Baptist Church in Mobile, Alabama. He and his wife, Jane, have one son, Aidan.

Kurt Gebhards shepherds The Foundry (Grace Church's ministry to single adults in their twenties and thirties) as well as directing Logos Equipping Ministries (Grace Church's Bible institute for laymen). Kurt earned his Master of Divinity degree in 2001 and his Master of Theology degree in 2004, both from The Master's Seminary. Kurt and his wife, Julie, have three children—Reilly, Shea, and McKinley.

Daniel Gillespie is the director of the Shepherds' Conference (Grace Church's annual pastors' conference) and the Expositor's Institute (Grace Church's annual finishing school for preachers). Before moving to California, Daniel was involved in campus ministry at North Carolina State University. Daniel graduated from the Master's Seminary in 2004. He and his wife, Lisa, have one son, Jacob.

Carey Hardy serves as senior executive pastor at Grace Community Church and personal assistant to John MacArthur. He also pastors the Mainstream fellowship group (a ministry to young marrieds and families). In addition, he is an adjunct professor at The Master's College and Seminary, having graduated from The Master's Seminary in 1996. Before coming to Grace Church, Carey was a Christian school principal and minister of music in Texas. He and his wife, Pam, have four children—Christen, Nathan, Luke, and Catherine.

Rick Holland is the director of student ministries as well as the college pastor at Grace Community Church. He has served in youth ministry for twenty-two years and teaches as an adjunct professor of youth ministries at The Master's College. He is also the director of the Doctor of Ministries program at The Master's Seminary. Having earned his Master of Divinity degree from The Master's Seminary (1994), Rick completed his doctoral studies at The Southern Baptist Theological Seminary (D.Min.) in 2003. Rick and his wife, Kim, have three sons—Luke, John, and Mark.

Phil Johnson is the executive director of "Grace to You" (the Christian tape and radio ministry of John MacArthur) as well as the pastor of the Grace Life fellowship group (a ministry to families at Grace Church). In addition, he is the executive editor of *Pulpit*, the online magazine of the Shepherds' Fellowship. Phil has been closely associated with John MacArthur's ministry since 1981 and edits most of his major books. Before moving to California, Phil was an associate pastor in Florida and an editor for Moody Press. Phil and his wife, Darlene, have three sons—Jeremiah, Jedidiah, and Jonathan.

John MacArthur has been pastor-teacher of Grace Community Church since 1969. He is president of The Master's College and Seminary, is heard daily on "Grace to You," a nationally syndicated radio broadcast, and has authored nearly 100 books. He and his wife, Patricia, have four children (Matthew, Marcy, Mark, and Melinda) and thirteen grandchildren.

EDITOR'S INTRODUCTION

John MacArthur

A WOMAN ONCE WROTE ME to say she thought Christianity was fine, but personally she was "into Zen." She liked to listen to Christian radio while she was driving because the music "smoothed out her karma." Occasionally, however, she would tune in one of the Bible-teaching ministries. In her opinion, all the preachers she heard were too narrow-minded toward other religions, so she was writing several radio ministers to encourage them to be more broad-minded.

"God doesn't care *what* you believe, as long as you're sincere," she wrote, echoing an opinion I have heard many times. "All religions lead ultimately to the same reality. It doesn't matter which road you take to get there, as long as you follow your chosen road faithfully. Don't be critical of the alternative roads other people choose."

To those who accept the Bible as God's Word, the folly of that thinking should be immediately evident. If the consequences of what we believe mean the difference between right and wrong, God's pleasure and His punishment, life and death, then we must make sure that what we're believing is based on clear thinking. Put another way, we need to exercise discernment.

To be sure, discernment is about as fashionable to today's culture as absolute truth and humility. Making clear distinctions and judgments contradicts the relativistic values of modern culture. Pluralism and diversity have been enshrined as higher virtues than truth. We're not supposed to draw any definitive lines or declare any absolutes.

That is regarded as backward, outmoded, discourteous. And while this attitude toward biblical discernment is expected from the secular world, it is sadly being embraced by an increasing segment of evangelical Christianity.

As a result, evangelicalism is beginning to lose its distinctiveness—often choosing tolerance over truth. Not that most evangelicals would accept Islam, Hinduism, or other overtly non-Christian religions. But many seem to think it doesn't really matter what you believe, as long as you label it Christianity. With the exception of a few cults that blatantly renounce the Trinity, almost everything taught in the name of Christ is accepted by evangelicals—from Roman Catholicism (which denies that sinners are justified solely by faith) to the extreme charismatic Word Faith movement (which both corrupts the doctrine of Christ and makes temporal health and wealth the focus of salvation).

In the name of unity, such matters of doctrine are expressly *not* supposed to be contested. We are encouraged to insist on nothing more than a simple affirmation of faith in Jesus. Beyond that, the specific *content* of faith is supposed to be a matter of individual preference.

Of course, this general attitude of acceptance is not new; the church has waged an ongoing struggle over the issue of doctrinal discernment at least since the beginning of the twentieth century. This very same appeal for broad-mindedness in religious standards and beliefs has always been at the heart of the agenda of theological liberalism; indeed, it is precisely what the term *liberal* originally meant. What is new about today's appeals for tolerance is that they come from within the evangelical camp.

Nothing is more desperately needed in the church right now than a new movement to reemphasize the need for biblical discernment. Without such a movement, the true church is in serious trouble. If the current hunger for ecumenical compromise, pragmatic sanctification, and numerical success continues to gain a foothold within evangelicalism, it will result in an unmitigated spiritual disaster.

This book, then, is a plea for discernment. It is a reminder that God's truth is a precious commodity that must be handled carefully—not diluted with whimsical beliefs or bound up in human traditions. When churches, or individual Christians, lose their resolve to discern between sound doctrine and error, between good and evil, between truth and lies, they open themselves up to every kind of error. But those who apply biblical discernment consistently, in every area of life, are sure to walk in the wisdom of the Lord (Prov 2:1-6). In contrast, today's Christians soothe themselves with the opinion that few things are really black and white. Doctrinal issues, moral questions, and Christian principles are all cast in hues of gray. Every person is encouraged to do what is right in his own eyes—exactly what God forbade (cf. Deut 12:8; Judg 17:6; 21:25).

The church will never manifest its power in society until we regain a passionate love for truth and a corollary hatred for error. True Christians cannot condone or disregard anti-Christian influences in their midst and expect to enjoy God's blessing. "Besides this you know the time, that the hour has come for you to wake from sleep. For salvation is nearer to us now than when we first believed. The night is far gone; the day is at hand. So then let us cast off the works of darkness and put on the armor of light" (Rom 13:11-12). Thus, "it is my prayer that your love may abound more and more, with knowledge and all discernment, so that you may approve what is excellent, and so be pure and blameless for the day of Christ, filled with the fruit of righteousness that comes through Jesus Christ, to the glory and praise of God" (Phil 1:9-11).

PART ONE

Promoting Discernment in an Age of Blind Acceptance

1

ALL THAT GLITTERS . . .: A CALL FOR BIBLICAL DISCERNMENT[1]

John MacArthur

This chapter lays the foundation for biblical discernment—a foundation that is of crucial importance, and yet often overlooked in our postmodern culture. Each subsequent chapter in this book builds on this foundation, applying the principles found here to a number of current Christian trends. In an age of open-mindedness, too many believers have forfeited biblical clarity and exchanged it for a life of confusion and compromise. They accept too much with too little discernment. But God's Word makes it clear that not everything that glitters is true gold; doctrinal error abounds at every turn, the temptation to embrace it is great, and the stakes involved are eternal. God calls us, as His people, to distinguish what's good from what's bad. And that's why we need biblical discernment.

Eureka!

It is a simple Greek word, only six letters long. But for a generation of treasure seekers in the late 1840s, it became a life slogan. Meaning "I have found it!" in English, the term purportedly comes from Archimedes, the Greek mathematician who cried out "Eureka! Eureka!" when he determined how much gold was in King Hiero's crown. Yet, for James Marshall (who discovered gold at Sutter's Mill in 1848) and many of his contemporaries, the term took on new meaning. For them, "eureka" meant instant riches, early retirement, and a life of carefree ease. It's no wonder California (the "Golden State") includes this term on its official seal, along with the picture of a zealous gold miner.

News of Marshall's discovery spread quickly throughout the nation. By 1850 over 75,000 hopefuls had traveled to California by land, and another 40,000 by sea. Whether by wagon or by boat, the journey was an arduous one, as adventurers left friends and family behind in search of vast fortunes. Even when they finally arrived in San Francisco, the closest goldfields were still 150 miles away. Undaunted nonetheless, many of the forty-niners set up mining camps and started to dig.

As they traveled out to their various destinations, prospectors quickly learned that not everything that looked like gold actually was. Riverbeds and rock quarries could be full of golden specks, and yet entirely worthless. This "fool's gold" was iron pyrite, and miners had to be able to distinguish it from the real thing. Their very livelihood depended on it.

Experienced miners could usually distinguish pyrite from gold simply by looking at it. But in some cases the distinction was not quite so clear. So they developed tests to discern what was genuine from what wasn't. One test involved biting the rock in question. Real gold is softer than the human tooth, while fool's gold is harder. A broken tooth meant that a prospector needed to keep digging. A second test involved scraping the rock on a piece of white stone, such as ceramic. True gold leaves a yellow streak, while the residue left by fool's gold is greenish-black. In either case, a miner relied on tests to authenticate his finds—both his fortune and his future depended on the results.

Doctrinally speaking, today's church is in a similar position to the California gold rushers of 1850. Spiritual riches are promised at every turn. New programs, new philosophies, new parachurch ministries—each glitters a little bit more than the last, promising better results and bigger returns. But, as was true in the mid-1800s, just because it glitters doesn't mean it's good. Christians need to be equally wary of "fool's gold." We must not accept new trends (or old traditions) without first testing them to see if they meet with God's approval. If they fail the test, we should discard them and warn others also. But if they pass the test, in keeping with the truth of God's Word, we can embrace and endorse them wholeheartedly.

California gold miners would only cry "Eureka!" when they found true gold. As Christians, we should be careful to do the same.

OUR NEED FOR DISCERNMENT

In considering nineteenth-century miners, we are reminded of the need to discriminate between truth and falsehood. In modern usage, the word *discrimination* carries powerful negative connotations. But the word itself is not negative. *Discriminate* simply means "to make a clear distinction." We used to call someone "a discriminating person" if he or she exercised keen judgment. "Discrimination" signified a positive ability to draw the line between good and evil, true and false, right and wrong. In the heyday of the American civil rights movement the word was widely applied to racial bigotry. And, indeed, people who make unfair distinctions between races are guilty of an evil form of discrimination.

Unfortunately, the word itself took on that negative connotation, and the sinister implication is often transferred to anyone who tries to discriminate in any way. To view homosexuality as immoral (1 Cor 6:9-10; 1 Tim 1:9-10) is condemned now by the politically correct as an unacceptable form of discrimination. To suggest that wives ought to submit to their own husbands (Eph 5:22; Col 3:18) is now classified as unfair discrimination. To suggest that children ought to obey their parents (Eph 6:1) is also labeled unjust discrimination by some. Anyone who "discriminates" in these ways risks becoming a target of lawsuits by the ACLU.

The idea of discrimination itself has fallen out of favor. We are not supposed to draw lines. We are not supposed to discriminate.

That is the spirit of this age, and unfortunately, it has crept into the church.

If we are going to be discerning people, we must develop the skill of discriminating between truth and error, good and bad. The original languages of Scripture convey this very idea. The main Hebrew word for "discernment" is *bin*. The word and its variants are used hundreds of times in the Old Testament. It is often translated "discernment," "understanding," "skill," or "carefulness." But in the original language it conveys the same idea as our word *discrimination*. It entails the idea of making distinctions. Jay Adams points out that the word *bin* "is related to the noun *bayin*, which means 'interval' or 'space between,' and the preposition *ben*, 'between.' In essence it means to separate things from one another at their points of difference in order to distinguish them."[2] *Discernment*, then, is a synonym for *discrimination*. In fact, the Greek verb translated "discern" in the New Testament is *diakrinō*. It means, "to make a distinction" and is literally translated that way in Acts 15:9.

So discernment is the process of making careful distinctions in our thinking about truth. The discerning person is the one who draws a clear contrast between truth and error. Discernment is black-and-white thinking—the conscious refusal to color every issue in shades of gray. No one can be truly discerning without developing skill in separating divine truth from error.

Does Scripture tell us *how* to be discerning? It certainly does. Paul sums up the process in 1 Thessalonians 5:21-22: "test everything; hold fast what is good. Abstain from every form of evil." There, in three straightforward commands, he spells out the requirements of a discerning mind.

JUDGE EVERYTHING

Let's quickly set the context for this passage. Starting with verse 16, Paul lists some very brief reminders to the Thessalonian Christians. These might be thought of as the basics of Christian living: "Rejoice always, pray without ceasing, give thanks in all circumstances; for this is the will of God in Christ Jesus for you. Do not quench the Spirit. Do not despise prophecies." Rejoicing, prayer, contentment, responsiveness to the preaching of God's Word—those are all primary duties of every Christian.

Another duty is discernment. "Test everything" (v. 21) is a call to discernment. It is significant that Paul sets discernment in a context of very basic commands. It is as crucial to the effective Christian life as prayer and contentment.

That may surprise some Christians who see discernment as uniquely a pastoral responsibility. It is certainly true that pastors and elders have an even greater duty to be discerning than the average layperson. Most of the calls to discernment in the New Testament are issued to church leaders (1 Tim 4:6-7, 13, 16; Titus 1:9). Every elder is required to be skilled in teaching truth and able to refute unsound doctrine. As a pastor, I am constantly aware of this responsibility. Everything I read, for example, goes through a grid of discrimination in my mind. If you were to look through my library, you would instantly be able to identify which books I have read. The margins are marked. Sometimes you'll see approving remarks and heavy underlining. Other times you'll find question marks—or even red lines through the text. I constantly strive to separate truth from error. I read that way, I think that way, and of course I preach that way. My passion is to know the truth and proclaim it with authority. That should be the passion of every elder, because everything we teach affects the hearts and lives of those who hear us. It is an awesome responsibility. Any church leader who does not feel the burden of this duty ought to step down from leadership.

But discernment is not *only* the duty of pastors and elders. The same careful discernment Paul demanded of pastors and elders is also the duty of every Christian. First Thessalonians 5:21 is written to the *entire church*: "Examine everything carefully" (NASB).

The Greek text is by no means complex. The word "carefully" has been added by the translators to make the sense clear. If we translate the phrase literally, we find it simply says, "Examine everything." But the idea conveyed by our word *carefully* is included in the Greek word translated "examine," *dokimazō*. This is a familiar word in the New Testament. Elsewhere it is translated "analyze," "test," or "prove." It refers to the process of testing something to reveal its genuineness, such as in the testing of precious metals. Paul is urging believers to scrutinize everything they hear to see that it is genuine, to distinguish between the true and the false, to separate the good from the evil. In other words, he wants them to examine everything *critically*. "Test everything," he is saying. "Judge everything."

Wait a minute. What about Matthew 7:1 ("Judge not, that you be not judged")? Typically someone will quote that verse and suggest that it rules out any kind of critical or analytical appraisal of what others believe. Was Jesus forbidding Christians from judging what is taught in His name?

Obviously not. The spiritual discernment Paul calls for is different from the judgmental attitude Jesus forbade. In Matthew 7, Jesus went on to say,

> For with the judgment you pronounce you will be judged, and with the measure you use it will be measured to you. Why do you see the speck that is in your brother's eye, but do not notice the log that is in your own eye? Or how can you say to your brother, "Let me take the speck out of your eye," when there is the log in your own eye? You hypocrite, first take the log out of your own eye, and then you will see clearly to take the speck out of your brother's eye. (vv. 2-5)

Obviously, what Jesus condemned was the hypocritical judgment of those who held others to a higher standard than they themselves were willing to live by. He was certainly not suggesting that *all* judgment is forbidden. In fact, Jesus indicated that taking a speck out of your brother's eye is the *right* thing to do—if you first get the log out of your own eye.

Elsewhere in Scripture we are forbidden to judge others' motives or attitudes. We are not able to discern "the thoughts and intentions of the heart" (Heb 4:12). That is a divine prerogative. Only God can judge the heart, because only God can see it (1 Sam 16:7). He alone knows the secrets of the heart (Ps 44:21). He alone can weigh the motives (Prov 16:2). And He alone "will judge the secrets of men through Christ Jesus" (Rom 2:16). That is not our role. "Therefore do not pronounce judgment before the time, before the Lord comes, who will bring to light the things now hidden in darkness and will disclose the purposes of the heart" (1 Cor 4:5).

What is forbidden is hypocritical judging and judging others' thoughts and motives. But other forms of judgment are explicitly commanded. Throughout Scripture the people of God are urged to judge between truth and error, right and wrong, good and evil. Jesus said, "Judge with right judgment" (John 7:24). Paul wrote to the Corinthian believers, "I speak as to sensible people; judge for yourselves what I say" (1 Cor 10:15). Clearly, God *requires* us to be discriminating when it comes to matters of sound doctrine.

We are also supposed to judge one another with regard to overt acts of sin. Paul wrote, "Is it not those inside the church whom you are to judge? God judges those outside. 'Purge the evil person from among you'" (1 Cor 5:12-13). That speaks of the same process of discipline outlined by Jesus Himself in Matthew 18:15-20.

At least one other kind of judgment is expressly required of every believer. We must examine and judge our own selves: "if we judged ourselves truly, we would not be judged" (1 Cor 11:31). This calls for a careful searching and judging of our own hearts. Paul called for this self-examination every time we partake of the Lord's Supper (v. 28). All other righteous forms of judgment depend on this honest self-examination. That is what Jesus meant when He said, "first take the log out of your own eye" (Luke 6:42).

Clearly, then, the command in 1 Thessalonians 5:21, "Test everything," in no way contradicts the biblical strictures against being judgmental. The discernment called for here is *doctrinal* discernment. The conjunction at the beginning of this verse—"*but* test everything"— ties it to the "prophecies" mentioned in verse 20.

A prophecy was not necessarily a new revelation. The gift of prophecy in the New Testament has to do more with *proclaiming* the

Word of God than with *obtaining* it. In the context of this passage, it
clearly has to do with any spiritual message that the Thessalonians
received—any message that claimed to carry divine approval or
authority.

The unusually gullible Thessalonians seemed to have a problem in this regard. Like many today, they were eager to believe
whatever was preached in the name of Christ. They were undis-
criminating. That's why Paul addresses this continual lack of discernment in both of his Thessalonian epistles. There is evidence in
the first epistle, for example, that someone had confused the
Thessalonians about the return of Christ. They were going through
a time of severe persecution, and apparently some of them thought
they had missed the Second Coming. In chapter 3 we learn that
Paul had sent Timothy from Athens specifically to strengthen and
encourage them in their faith (v. 2). They were unaccountably confused about why they were being persecuted. Paul had to remind
them, "you yourselves know that we are destined for this. For when
we were with you, we kept telling you beforehand that we were to
suffer affliction" (vv. 3-4). Evidently someone had also taught them
that believers who died before the Second Coming of Christ would
miss that event entirely. They were in serious confusion. Chapters
4—5 contain Paul's efforts to correct that confusion. He tells them
that the dead in Christ will rise and be caught up with the living
(4:16-17). And he assures them that although that day will come
like a thief in the night (5:2), they need not fear being caught off
guard (vv. 3-6).

Incredibly, shortly after this, Paul had to write a second epistle,
again assuring the Thessalonians that they had not missed some great
event on the prophetic calendar. Someone, it seems, had sent them a
counterfeit epistle claiming to be from Paul and suggesting that the
day of the Lord had come already. They should not have been duped
by such a ploy because Paul had written so plainly in his first epistle.
He wrote them again: "Now concerning the coming of our Lord
Jesus Christ and our being gathered together to him, we ask you,
brothers, not to be quickly shaken in mind or alarmed, either by a

spirit or a spoken word, or a letter seeming to be from us, to the effect that the day of the Lord has come. Let no one deceive you" (2 Thess 2:1-3). There was no excuse for their chronic gullibility.

Why were they so vulnerable to false teaching? Surely it was precisely because they lacked biblical discernment. The Thessalonians did not examine everything in light of God's Word. If they had, they would not have been so easily hoodwinked. And that is why Paul urged them, "Test everything."

It is fair to point out that the Thessalonians were at a disadvantage compared to Christians today. They did not have all the written books of New Testament Scripture. Paul wrote these two epistles to Thessalonica very early in the New Testament era—about A.D. 51. The two letters were probably written only a few months apart and are among the very earliest of all the New Testament writings. The Thessalonians' primary source of authoritative gospel truth was Paul's teaching. As an apostle, Paul taught with absolute authority. When he taught them, his message *was* the Word of God, and he commended them for recognizing that: "And we also thank God constantly for this, that when you received the word of God, which you heard from us, you accepted it not as the word of men but as what it really is, the word of God, which is at work in you believers" (1 Thess 2:13). Elsewhere he said that the commandments he gave them were by the authority of the Lord Jesus (4:2).

The *substance* of what he taught them represented the same body of truth that is available to us in the New Testament Scriptures. How do we know? Paul himself said so. Even as he was recording his inspired epistle to them, he reminded them, "Do you not remember that when I was still with you I told you these things?" (2 Thess 2:5). The written Word simply confirmed and recorded for all time the authoritative truth he had already taught them in person. These epistles were a written reminder of what they had already heard from Paul's own mouth (1 Thess 4:2).

Second Thessalonians 2:15 confirms this: "stand firm and hold to the traditions that you were taught by us, either by our spoken word or by our letter." There he declares, first of all, that his epistles to them are authoritative, inspired truth. This verse is a clear statement that Paul himself regarded these epistles as inspired Scripture.

But notice also that this verse joins the apostolic "traditions" with the written Word of God. The "traditions" necessary for Christians to be discerning are recorded for all ages in the text of Scripture. Those who claim that apostolic tradition is *other* truth *in addition to* Scripture often attempt to use this verse for support. Note, however, that Paul is not saying "the traditions [they] were taught" are *different* from the written Scriptures. Rather he links the two, affirming that the written Word of God is the only permanent and authoritative record of the apostolic tradition. He is specifically suggesting that the Thessalonians should not trust "word of mouth" or letters pretending to be from apostolic sources. Only what they had heard firsthand from Paul's own lips or read in authentic letters from him were they to treat as authoritative divine truth. That is why Paul usually signed his epistles "with [his] own hand" (1 Cor 16:21; Gal 6:11; Col 4:18; 2 Thess 3:17; Philem 19).

With this in mind, 2 Thessalonians 2:15 cannot be used to support the claim that extrabiblical, spiritually binding "apostolic tradition" is passed down verbally through popes and bishops. Paul's whole point was that the Thessalonians should treat as authoritative only what they had heard from his own mouth or received from his own pen. That body of truth—the Word of God—was to be the measuring stick they used to examine all things. Two other verses confirm this. In 2 Thessalonians 3:6 Paul writes, "Now we command you, brothers, in the name of our Lord Jesus Christ, that you keep away from any brother who is walking in idleness and not in accord with the tradition that you received from us." And in verse 14 he adds, "If anyone does not obey what we say in this letter, take note of that person, and have nothing to do with him, that he may be ashamed."

Therefore, Paul is affirming that the Bible is the only reliable criterion by which believers in this age can evaluate any message claiming to be truth from God.

CLING TO WHAT IS GOOD

The testing of truth Paul calls for is not merely an academic exercise. It demands an active, twofold response. First there is a positive response to whatever is good: "Hold fast what is good" (1 Thess 5:21). This is an echo of Romans 12:9: "Abhor what is evil; hold fast to what is good." The expressions "hold fast" or "cling to" (NASB) speak of jealously safeguarding the truth. Paul is calling for the same careful watchfulness he demanded of Timothy every time he wrote him: "O Timothy, guard the deposit entrusted to you" (1 Tim 6:20); "Follow the pattern of the sound words that you have heard from me. . . . By the Holy Spirit who dwells within us, guard the good deposit entrusted to you" (2 Tim 1:13-14). In other words, the truth is given into our custody, and we are charged with guarding it against every possible threat.

This describes a militant, defensive, protective stance against anything that undermines the truth or does violence to it in any way. We must hold the truth securely, defend it zealously, preserve it from all threats. To placate the enemies of truth or lower our guard is to violate this command.

"Hold fast" also carries the idea of embracing something. It goes beyond bare assent to "that which is good" and speaks of loving the truth wholeheartedly. Those who are truly discerning are passionately committed to sound doctrine, to truth, and to all that is inspired by God.

Every true Christian has this quality to some degree. Paul even defined salvation as "lov[ing] the truth" (2 Thess 2:10), and he told the Corinthians they proved their salvation by holding fast to the gospel he had delivered (1 Cor 15:2). Those who utterly fail to hold fast to the saving message are those who have "believed in vain"; that is, their faith was empty to begin with. The apostle John said something similar: "They went out from us, but they were not of us; for if they had been of us, they would have continued with us. But they went out, that it might become plain that they all are not of us" (1 John 2:19). All true believers hold fast to the gospel.

Paul was urging the Thessalonians to nurture and cultivate their love for truth, to let it rule their thinking. He wanted them to foster a conscious commitment to *all* truth, a faithfulness to sound doctrine, a pattern of holding fast to all that is good.

The attitude this calls for is incompatible with the suggestion that we should lay doctrine aside for the sake of unity. It cannot be reconciled with the opinion that hard truths should be downplayed to make God's Word more palatable for unbelievers. It is contrary to the notion that personal experience takes precedence over objective truth. God has given us His truth objectively in His Word. It is a treasure that we should protect at all costs.

This is the opposite of undiscerning faith. Paul leaves no room for rote tradition. He makes no place for a blind, irrational faith that refuses to consider the authenticity of its object and just accepts at face value everything that claims to be true. He rules out the kind of "faith" that is driven by feelings, emotion, and the human imagination. Instead, we are to identify "what is good" by examining everything carefully, objectively, rationally—using Scripture as our standard.

No human teacher, no personal experience, no strong feeling is exempt from this objective test. Jay Adams writes, "If inspired prophecies in the apostolic age had to be subjected to testing . . . then surely the teachings of men today should also be put to the test."[3] Indeed, if the words of prophets in apostolic times needed to be examined and evaluated, then surely we ought to subject the words of self-proclaimed "prophets" and preachers today to even more intense scrutiny in the bright light of the completed New Testament. The same is true of every subjective experience and every emotion. Experience and feelings—no matter how powerful—do not determine what is true. Rather, those things themselves must be subjected to the test.

"That which is good" is truth that accords with God's Word. The word "good" is *kalos*, meaning something that is inherently good. It isn't just something that is fair to look at, lovely or beautiful in appearance. This speaks of something good in itself—genuine, true, noble, right, and good. In other words, "that which is good" does not refer to that which is entertaining. It does not refer to that which garners accolades from the world. It does not refer to that which is satisfying to the flesh. It refers to that which is good, true, accurate, authentic, dependable—that which is in agreement with the infallible Word of God. When you find such truth, embrace it and guard it like a treasure.

ʃHUN WHAT Iʃ EVIL

The other side of Paul's command is a negative response to evil: "Abstain from every form of evil" (1 Thess 5:22). The word translated "abstain" is a very strong verb, *apechō*, meaning "hold oneself back," "keep away from," "shun." It is the same word used in 1 Thessalonians 4:3, "abstain from sexual immorality," and 1 Peter 2:11, "abstain from the passions of the flesh." It calls for a radical separation from "every form of evil." This would include evil behavior, of course. But in this context, the primary reference seems to be evil teaching—false doctrine. Having examined everything in light of God's Word, when you identify something that does not measure up—something that is evil, untrue, erroneous, or contrary to sound doctrine—shun it.

Scripture does not give believers permission to expose themselves to evil. Some people believe the only way to defend against false doctrine is to study it, become proficient in it, and master all its nuances—then refute it. I know people who study the cults more than they study sound doctrine. Some Christians immerse themselves in the philosophy, entertainment, and culture of society. They feel such a strategy will strengthen their witness to unbelievers.

But the emphasis of that strategy is all wrong. Our focus should be on knowing the *truth*. Error is to be shunned.

Granted, we cannot recede into a monastic existence to escape exposure to every evil influence. But neither are we supposed to be experts about evil. The apostle Paul wrote, "I want you to be wise as to what is good and innocent as to what is evil" (Rom 16:19).

Federal agents don't learn to spot counterfeit money by studying the counterfeits. They study genuine bills until they master the look of the real thing. Then when they see bogus money they recognize it. Detecting a spiritual counterfeit requires the same discipline. Master the truth to refute error. Don't spend time studying error; shun it. Study truth. Hold fast the faithful Word. Then you will be able both to exhort in sound doctrine and to refute those who contradict (Titus 1:9). As Paul wrote elsewhere, "Do not be overcome by evil, but overcome evil with good" (Rom 12:21).

In the King James Version, 1 Thessalonians 5:22 is translated "abstain from all *appearance* of evil." The word translated "appearance" is *eidos*, literally "that which is seen." The *New American Standard Bible* and *English Standard Version* translation, "every *form* of evil," gives the better sense. We are to reject evil however it appears, to shun every manifestation of it.

This explicitly rules out *syncretism*. Syncretism is the practice of blending ideas from different religions and philosophies. I remember meeting a man once who compared his view of spirituality to a quilt—different ideas from different religions made up his own personal patchwork of faith. He devoured materials from every cult and denomination, looking for good in all of it. Whatever he deemed good, he absorbed for his belief system. He was designing his own unique religion based on syncretism.

That man might attempt to use 1 Thessalonians 5:21 to justify his methodology: "test everything; hold fast what is good." That is, after all, precisely what he thought he was doing. But he was actually doing the opposite of what this passage demands. Verse 21 is balanced by verse 22: "Abstain from every form of evil."

The only proper response to false teaching is to shun it. Erroneous doctrine is no place to look for truth. There is usually *some* point of truth even in rank heresy. But it is truth out of balance, corrupted truth, truth mixed with lies and therefore rendered dangerous. Shun it.

Satan is subtle. He often sabotages the truth by mixing it with error. Truth mixed with error is usually far more effective and far more destructive than a straightforward contradiction of the truth.

If you think everything you read or hear on Christian radio and television is reliable teaching, then you are a prime target for doctrinal deception. If you think everyone who *appears* to love the truth really does, then you don't understand the wiles of Satan. "Satan disguises himself as an angel of light," Paul wrote. "So it is no surprise if his servants, also, disguise themselves as servants of righteousness" (2 Cor 11:14-15).

Satan also disguises his lies as truth. He doesn't always wage war openly against the gospel. He is much more likely to attack the church by infiltrating with subtle error. He uses the Trojan horse stratagem by placing his false teachers *in the church*, where they can "secretly bring in destructive heresies" (2 Pet 2:1). He puts his lies in the mouth of someone who claims to speak for Jesus Christ—someone likable and appealing; then he spreads his perverse lies in the church where they can draw away Christ's disciples (Acts 20:30). He attaches Bible verses to his lies (Matt 4:6). He uses deception and hypocrisy. He disguises falsehood as truth. He loves syncretism. It makes evil *look* good.

That's why we are to examine *everything* carefully and shun whatever is unsound, corrupt, or erroneous. It is deadly. Millions in the church today are being overwhelmed by the Trojan-horse ploy calling for the integration of secular ideas with biblical truth. Others are easily duped by anything labeled Christian. They don't examine everything. They don't hold fast to the truth. And they won't shun evil. They are left vulnerable to false doctrine and have no defense against theological confusion.

THE REAJON FOR THIJ BOOK

The apostle Paul's clear teaching in 1 Thessalonians 5:21-22 cannot simply be avoided or ignored. As in the days of the early church, doctrinal error is all around us. Often it looks very good—that's why so many fall prey to its deception. And that is also why God gave us His Word, so that we would have a measuring stick by which to examine every spiritual or theological message we encounter.

In the ensuing chapters, this book will address several contemporary Christian issues in light of God's revealed truth. The goal in doing so is not to be unloving, but rather to preserve that which is "first pure, then peaceable" (Jas 3:17). In fact, Scripture makes it clear that this type of examination is inherently loving, as God's people are called to think biblically and exercise discernment. To do anything less will only result in spiritual anemia (cf. Hos 4:6).

My prayer for you, as you encounter any doctrinal teaching, is that you would be like the Bereans who were more noble because they were "examining the Scriptures daily to see if these things were so" (Acts 17:11).

2

PLEXIGLAS PREACHING: THE DEVASTATING CONSEQUENCES OF A WATERED-DOWN MESSAGE

John MacArthur

Having established the importance of discernment in Chapter 1, this chapter addresses its absence in contemporary Christianity. It is an examination of the major reasons discernment is so scarce in today's church. The culprit is watered-down preaching. Hosea 4:6 records God's estimation of spiritual leaders who fail to faithfully proclaim His message: "My people are destroyed for lack of knowledge; because you have rejected knowledge, I reject you from being a priest to me." A quick survey of modern preaching reveals that many contemporary pulpits deserve similar assessments. Why? It is because they have exchanged the full counsel of God for doctrinally shallow, seeker-friendly "talks." When warm and fuzzy moral messages, peppered with cute anecdotes and an occasional skit, replace the meat of God's Word, the consequences are devastating. This chapter, which originally appeared as an article in Pulpit *magazine, outlines the disastrous results of Plexiglas pulpits and the messages they represent.*

Those who are familiar with my ministry know that I am committed to expository preaching. It is my unshakable conviction that the proclamation of God's Word should always be the heart and the focus of the church's ministry (2 Tim 4:2). And proper biblical preaching should be systematic, expositional, theological, and God-centered.

Such preaching is in short supply these days. There are plenty of gifted communicators in the modern evangelical movement, but today's sermons tend to be short, shallow, topical homilies that massage people's egos and focus on fairly insipid subjects like human relationships, "successful" living, emotional issues, and other practical but worldly—and not definitively *biblical*—themes. Like the ubiquitous Plexiglas lecterns from which these messages are delivered, such preaching is lightweight and without substance, cheap and synthetic, leaving little more than an ephemeral impression on the minds of the hearers.

Some time ago I hosted a discussion at the Expositors' Institute, an annual small-group colloquium on preaching held at our church. In preparation for that seminar, I took a yellow legal pad and a pen and began listing the negative effects of the superficial brand of preaching that is so rife in modern evangelicalism.

I initially thought I might be able to identify about ten, but in the end I had jotted down a list of sixty-one devastating consequences. I've distilled them to fifteen by combining and eliminating all but the most crucial ones. I offer them as a warning against superficial, marginally-biblical preaching—both to those who stand behind the pulpit and to those who sit in the pew.

1. It usurps the authority of God over the soul. Whether a preacher boldly proclaims the Word of God or not is ultimately a question of authority. Who has the right to speak to the church? The preacher or God? Whenever *anything* is substituted for the preaching of the Word, God's authority is usurped. What a prideful thing to do! In fact, it is hard to conceive of anything more insolent that could be done by a man who is called by God to preach.

2. It removes the lordship of Christ from His church. Who is the Head of the church? Is Christ really the dominant teaching authority in the church? If so, then why are there so many churches where His Word is not being faithfully proclaimed? When we look at contemporary ministry, we see programs and methods that are the fruit of human invention, the offspring of opinion polls and neighborhood surveys, and other pragmatic artifices. Church-growth experts have in essence wrested control of the church's agenda from her true Head, the Lord Jesus Christ. Our Puritan forefathers resisted the imposition of government-imposed liturgies for precisely this reason: They saw it as a direct attack on the headship of Christ over His own church. Modern preachers who neglect the Word of God have yielded the ground those men fought and sometimes died for. When Jesus Christ is exalted among His people, His power is manifest in the church. When the church is commandeered by compromisers who want to appease the culture, the gospel is minimized, true power is lost, artificial energy must be manufactured, and superficiality takes the place of truth.

3. It hinders the work of the Holy Spirit. What is the instrument the Spirit uses to do His work? The Word of God. He uses the Word as the instrument of regeneration (1 Pet 1:23; Jas 1:18). He also uses it as the means of sanctification (John 17:17). In fact, it is the *only* tool He uses (Eph 6:17). So when preachers neglect God's Word, they undermine the work of the Holy Spirit, producing shallow conversions and spiritually lame Christians—if not utterly spurious ones.

4. It demonstrates appalling pride and a lack of submission. In the modern approach to "ministry," the Word of God is deliberately downplayed, the reproach of Christ is quietly repudiated, the offense of the gospel is carefully eliminated, and "worship" is purposely tailored to fit the preferences of unbelievers. That is nothing but a *refusal* to submit to the biblical mandate for the church. The effrontery of ministers who pursue such a course is, to me, frightening.

5. It severs the preacher personally from the regular sanctifying grace of Scripture. The greatest personal benefit that I get from preaching is the work that the Spirit of God does on my own soul as I study and prepare for two expository messages each Lord's day. Week by week the duty of careful exposition keeps my own heart focused and fixed on the Scriptures, and the Word of God nourishes me while I prepare to feed my flock. So I am personally blessed and spiritually strengthened through the enterprise. If for no other reason, I would never abandon biblical preaching. The enemy of our souls is after preachers in particular, and the sanctifying grace of the Word of God is critical to our protection.

6. It clouds the true depth and transcendence of our message and therefore cripples both corporate and personal worship. What passes for preaching in some churches today is literally no more profound than what preachers in our fathers' generation were teaching in the five-minute children's sermon they gave before dismissing the kids. That's no exaggeration. It is *often* that simplistic, if not utterly inane. There is nothing deep about it. Such an approach makes it impossible for true worship to take place, because worship is a transcendent experience. Worship should take us above the mundane and simplistic. So the only way true worship can occur is if we first come to grips with the depth of spiritual truth. Our people can only rise high in worship in the same proportion to which we have taken them deep into the profound truths of the Word. There is no way they can have lofty thoughts of God unless we have plunged them into the depths of God's self-revelation. But preaching today is neither profound nor transcendent. It doesn't go down, and it doesn't go up. It merely aims to entertain.

By the way, true worship is not something that can be stimulated artificially. A bigger, louder band and more sentimental music might do more to stir people's emotions. But that is not genuine worship. True worship is a response from the heart to God's *truth* (John 4:23). You can actually worship *without* music if you have seen the glories and the depth of what the Bible teaches.

7. It prevents the preacher from fully developing the mind of Christ. Pastors are supposed to be undershepherds of Christ. Too many modern preachers are so bent on understanding the culture that they develop the mind of the culture and not the mind of Christ. They start to think like the world, and not like the

Savior. Frankly, the nuances of worldly culture are virtually irrelevant to me. I want to know the mind of Christ and bring that to bear on the culture, no matter what culture I may be ministering to. If I'm going to stand up in a pulpit and be a representative of Jesus Christ, I want to know how *He* thinks—and that must be my message to His people too. The only way to know and proclaim the mind of Christ is by being faithful to study and preach His Word. What happens to preachers who obsess about cultural "relevancy" is that they become worldly, not godly.

8. It depreciates by example the spiritual duty and priority of personal Bible study. Is personal Bible study important? Of course. But what example does the preacher set when he neglects the Bible in his own preaching? Why would people think they need to study the Bible if the preacher doesn't do serious study himself in the preparation of his sermons? There is now a movement among some of the gurus of "seeker-sensitive" ministry to trim, as much as possible, all explicit references to the Bible from the sermon—and above all, don't ever ask your people to turn to a specific Bible passage because that kind of thing makes "seekers" uncomfortable. Some "seeker-sensitive" churches actively discourage their people from bringing Bibles to church lest the sight of so many Bibles intimidate the "seekers." As if it were dangerous to give your people the impression that the Bible might be important!

9. It prevents the preacher from being the voice of God on every issue of his time. Jeremiah 8:9 says, "The wise men are ashamed, they are dismayed and taken. Behold, they have rejected the word of the Lord; so what wisdom do they have?" When I speak, I want to be *God's* messenger. I'm not interested in exegeting what some psychologist or business guru or college professor has to say about an issue. My people don't need my opinion; they need to hear what *God* has to say. If we preach as Scripture commands us, there should be no ambiguity about whose message is coming from the pulpit.

10. It breeds a congregation that is as weak and indifferent to the glory of God as their pastor is. "Seeker-sensitive" preaching fosters people who are consumed with their own well-being. When you tell people that the church's primary ministry is to fix for them whatever is wrong in this life—to meet their needs, to help them cope with their worldly disappointments, and so on—the message you are sending is that their mundane problems are more important than the glory of God and the majesty of Christ. Again, that sabotages true worship.

11. It robs people of their only true source of help. People who sit under superficial preaching become dependent on the cleverness and the creativity of the speaker. When preachers punctuate their sermons with laser lights and smoke, video clips and live drama, the message they send is that there isn't a prayer the people in the pew could ever extract such profound material on their own. Such gimmicks create a kind of dispensing mechanism that people can't use to serve themselves. So they become spiritual couch potatoes who just come in to be entertained, and whatever superficial spiritual content they get from the preacher's weekly performance is *all* they will get. They have no particular interest in the Bible because the sermons they hear don't cultivate that. They are wowed by the preacher's creativity and manipulated by the music, and that becomes their whole perspective on spirituality.

12. It encourages people to become indifferent to the Word of God and divine authority. Predictably, in a church where the preaching of Scripture is neglected, it becomes impossible to get people to submit to the authority of Scripture. The preacher who always aims at meeting felt needs and strokes the conceit of worldly people has no platform from which to confront the man who wants to divorce his wife without cause. The man will say, "You don't understand what I *feel*. I came here because you promised to meet my felt needs. And I'm telling you, I don't feel like I want to live with this woman anymore." You can't inject biblical authority into that. You certainly wouldn't have an easy time pursuing church discipline. That is the monster that superficial preaching creates. But if you are going to try to deal with sin and apply any kind of authoritative principle to keep the church pure, you *must* be preaching the Word.

13. It lies to people about what they really need. In Jeremiah 8:11, God condemns the prophets who treated people's wounds superficially. That verse applies powerfully to the plastic preachers who populate so many prominent evangelical pulpits today. They omit the hard truths about sin and judgment. They tone down the offensive parts of Christ's message. They lie to people about what they really need, promising them "fulfillment" and earthly well-being when what people really need is an exalted vision of Christ and a true understanding of the splendor of God's holiness.

14. It strips the pulpit of power. "The word of God is living and powerful, and sharper than any two-edged sword" (Heb 4:12). Everything else is impotent, giving merely an illusion of power. Human strategy is not more important than Scripture. The showman's ability to lure people in should not impress us more than the Bible's ability to transform lives.

15. It puts the responsibility on the preacher to change people with his cleverness. Preachers who pursue the modern approach to ministry must think they have the power to change people. That, too, is a frightening expression of pride. We preachers can't save people, and we can't sanctify them. We can't change people with our insights, our cleverness, by entertaining them or by appealing to their human whims and wishes and ambitions. There's only One who can change sinners. That's God, and He does it by His Spirit through the Word.

So pastors must preach the Word, even though it is currently out of fashion to do so (2 Tim 4:2). That is the only way their ministry can ever truly be fruitful. Moreover, it assures that they *will* be fruitful in ministry, because God's Word never returns to Him void; it always accomplishes that for which He sends it and prospers in what He sends it to do (Isa 55:11).

PART TWO

Practicing

Discernment

in Your

Local Bookstore

A SENSE OF PURPOSE: EVALUATING THE CLAIMS OF
The Purpose-Driven Life[1]

Nathan Busenitz

Outside the local church, there is probably no place in the community with more spiritual influence than the local Christian bookstore. For many believers, books provide the primary supplement to what is heard on Sundays. But just because something is on the shelf doesn't mean it is doctrinally accurate or spiritually beneficial. After all, biblical discernment is not just for sermons. It must also be applied to chapters and articles. Even best-sellers are not above the scrutiny of Scripture. This chapter compares the fastest-selling nonfiction book in history, The Purpose-Driven Life, *to the Word of Life—and assesses how the former measures up.*

With some 500,000 prepublication sales, *The Purpose-Driven Life* by Rick Warren was a mega-best-seller even before it was published. Its 2002 release was greeted with a groundswell of enthusiasm and anticipation as well-known evangelical leaders such as Billy Graham, Bruce Wilkinson, Max Lucado, and Lee Strobel gave glowing endorsements. Sales soon soared into the millions, and both *The New*

York Times and the Christian Booksellers Association quickly recognized its success. What began as the top-seller in its category has now become the best-seller of all best-sellers. As a marketing sensation, the book is undeniably an unprecedented phenomenon. Meanwhile, countless churches—both evangelical and otherwise—have joined Warren's "40 days of Purpose" campaign, and new ministries have been started to help churches after the forty days are over. In light of the response, it's not hard to see why the author believes he has ignited a new reformation.[2]

OVERVIEW

The Purpose-Driven Life claims to be "a guide to a 40-day spiritual journey that will enable you to discover the answer to life's most important question: What on earth am I here for?" (p. 9). Arguing that a forty-day period is the biblical precedent for life-change (p. 10), Warren answers the question "Why am I here?" by giving his readers five life-purposes:

1. You were planned for God's pleasure [Worship].
2. You were formed for God's family [Fellowship].
3. You were created to become like Christ [Spiritual Growth].
4. You were shaped for serving God [Spiritual Service].
5. You were made for a mission [Evangelism].

With this as the foundation, Warren systematically moves through his five areas of purpose—consistently showing his readers the benefits of living with those aims in mind. From this vantage point, *The Purpose-Driven Life* sounds pretty good. After all, what could be better than teaching millions of people about key biblical themes such as worship and spiritual growth?

We're certainly happy to see a major book from an evangelical publisher being read by hundreds of thousands who have never before been exposed to the claims of Christ. And we are glad the book has opened up many opportunities for Christians to talk about the

Lord with non-Christian friends and neighbors who had never thought seriously about spiritual things before.

But is this "ground-breaking manifesto on the meaning of life" (back cover) really all that it claims to be? Is *The Purpose-Driven Life* even the best tool for churches to use to introduce people to the basics of Christianity? Or are there some deficiencies in the message of the book that discerning Christians need to consider? With these questions in mind, let's look at some of the strengths and weaknesses of *The Purpose-Driven Life*.

STRENGTHS

It would be unfair to critique Rick Warren's best-selling work without first commending the book in several areas. For example, the book begins by asking an important question—namely, what is the purpose of life? This is the very question that Solomon wrestled with in Ecclesiastes, and it is a question that millions of people still struggle with today (as evidenced by the number of copies sold).

Not only does Warren start with an insightful question, but he also seeks to answer the question biblically. He correctly asserts that "it all starts with God" (p. 17), "it's all for him" (p. 53), "you were planned for God's pleasure" (p. 63), and "pleasing God is the first purpose of your life" (p. 69). Denouncing any type of "self-help" approach to Christianity, he argues instead that only God's Word can reveal what the true purpose of life is. "You must build your life on eternal truths," the author argues, "not pop psychology, success-motivation, or inspirational stories" (p. 20). For this reason, he references the Bible over 1,200 times—meaning that Scripture is cited an average of four times per page. Certainly, Warren's expressed desire to repeatedly appeal to God's Word is commendable.

The Purpose-Driven Life also surveys many key Christian themes—highlighting the importance of glorifying God (Day 7), developing a consistent devotional life (Days 11 and 25), loving other Christians (Day 16), ministering in the local church (Day 17), and witnessing to unbelievers (Day 37). In keeping with his five primary purposes (outlined above), Warren offers much practical wisdom for daily Christian living.

Warren's ability to communicate effectively is also one of *The Purpose-Driven Life's* clearest assets. From Day 1 to Day 40, the book is easy to read and easy to understand. Complete with clear illustrations, interesting call-outs, and helpful discussion questions, the format of *The Purpose-Driven Life* is incredibly user-friendly. As a result, its short chapters are less intimidating (and more accessible) for those who are new to evangelical literature.

From a Christian publishing point-of-view, Warren has accomplished what few authors are able to do—namely, produce a book that is deemed relevant by contemporary readers, yet is saturated with Scripture and, at the same time, easy to read and understand. On the basis of such strengths, it's no wonder *The Purpose-Driven Life* has been so well-received.

WEAHNEſſEſ

Of course, like any human book, *The Purpose-Driven Life* is not perfect. Yet, its incredible popularity has given it a place of influence that human works rarely enjoy. This prominence is especially significant since the book claims to offer its readers their very reason for existence. Thus, in light of both its popularity and subject-matter, *The Purpose-Driven Life* warrants careful examination from a biblical perspective.

It should be noted, from the outset, that the goal of this critique (in addressing several of the book's weaknesses) is not to suggest that *The Purpose-Driven Life* is heretical. At the same time, we believe it sets several dangerous precedents for its adherents. Our objective, then, is simply to advise readers of some of its perceived pitfalls.

1. A Casual Approach to Scripture

Our biggest concern with *The Purpose-Driven Life* is that although it frequently references the Bible, it often does so inaccurately. To be sure, Warren's initial claim sounds great: "The best way to explain

God's purpose for your life is to allow the Scripture to speak for itself, so in this book the Bible is quoted extensively" (p. 11). Further examination, however, reveals that *The Purpose-Driven Life* repeatedly quotes the Bible in an overly casual way.

With no less than fifteen different Bible translations and paraphrases, Warren offers proof-texts for much of his discussion, usually without any exegetical or contextual support. The author explains his reasons for this on page 325, contending that his "model for this is Jesus and how he and the apostles quoted the Old Testament. They often just quoted a phrase to make a point." Unfortunately, this thinking (which is debatable to begin with) allows Warren to pull passages completely out of context and apply them however he sees fit (using whatever loose paraphrase seems to agree with his argument). But unlike Jesus and the apostles, Warren is not inspired by the Holy Spirit—meaning he does not possess the authority to use God's Word however he pleases.

Several examples will suffice (although numerous instances could be given):

On page 19, Warren cites Matthew 16:25 from *The Message* paraphrase ("Self-help is no help at all. Self-sacrifice is the way, my way, to finding yourself, your true self") to argue that in order to be successful in life, you need more than self-help advice. Yet, a more literal translation of Matthew 16:25 quickly evidences that Christ is not talking about self-help advice in this context but rather about the essential nature of the saving gospel (ESV: "For whoever would save his life will lose it, but whoever loses his life for my sake will find it"). By not giving the context of the verse, and by using a very loose paraphrase, Warren changes the whole thrust of Jesus' statement.

On page 139, in speaking about fellowship in the church, Warren states, "God has made an incredible promise about small groups of believers: 'For where two or three have gathered together in My name, I am there in their midst [Matt 18:20].'" Yet, Matthew 18:20, in its context, has nothing to do with small-group fellowship in the church but rather with the church's authority in disciplining its members.

On page 165, the author encourages his readers not to spread or listen to gossip. He then says, "If you listen to gossip, God says you are a troublemaker. 'Troublemakers listen to troublemakers' [Prov 17:4]. 'These are the ones who split churches, thinking only of themselves' [Jude 16]." Yet Proverbs 17:4 does not directly mention gossip, and Jude 16 is not speaking of gossipers at all, but rather of false teachers (regarding their grumbling, pride, and flattery). While the point may be valid (that gossip is wrong), it cannot be honestly supported by arbitrarily combining Proverbs 17:4 with Jude 16. By handling those verses the way that he does (especially in the case of Jude 16), Warren fails to bring out the true meaning of the text.

In other places the author applies Old Testament passages directly to New Testament believers without any explanation of the original context or intended meaning. For example, Warren cites Jeremiah 29:11 when he says: "If you have felt hopeless hold on! Wonderful changes are going to happen in your life as you begin to live on purpose. God says, 'I know what I am planning for you. . . . I have good plans for you, not plans to hurt you. I will give you a hope and a good future'" (p. 31). The fact that this prophecy is actually given to Old Testament Israel with regard to the Babylonian Captivity is silently overlooked.

It doesn't take long to realize that this type of interpretive irresponsibility is destined for disaster. While the five life-purposes that Rick Warren explores in *The Purpose-Driven Life* are all biblical concepts, he does not always use the right texts to support his conclusions. Instead, he routinely picks and chooses whatever verse (or part of a verse) he wants, from whatever translation or paraphrase he thinks best makes his point. Doing so sets a dangerous example—implying to his readers that this type of Bible interpretation (where accuracy and context seem to be ignored) is perfectly acceptable

Even the premise of the book is based on a faulty interpretation of Scripture. Warren insists that a forty-day strategy is the best, most biblical way to instill significant spiritual change. He says, "The Bible is clear that God considers 40 days a spiritually significant time period. *Whenever* God wanted to prepare someone for his purposes, he took 40 days" (p. 9, emphasis added). Examples are then supplied, such as Noah (and the Flood), Moses (on Mount Sinai), the twelve spies (who spied on Canaan), David (and Goliath), Elijah (in the wilderness), the city of Nineveh (after Jonah preached to them), Jesus (in the wilderness), and the disciples (after the resurrection). The author's conclusion is unmistakable: God's preferred if not singular method of evoking life-change in His people is a forty-day program. And he adds this unqualified guarantee: "The next 40 days will transform your life" (p. 10).

But in claiming this, Warren has confused the *descriptive* with the *prescriptive*. Never are believers *commanded* to follow any forty-day program. To be fair, the number forty does seem to have some significance in Scripture, but it is never presented as a model we *must* follow.

Consider some of the examples Warren lists. The Flood was not a time in which Noah discovered his purpose in life. Rather, it was forty days of judgment on the earth. Noah had learned of his purpose 120 years earlier, when God commanded him to build the ark. The forty-day period Moses spent on Mount Sinai was also not a time of purpose-finding. Moses had already been given his purpose when he was commissioned by God at the burning bush. The twelve spies are also a poor example, especially since ten of them remained unchanged and unbelieving. David did not even hear about Goliath until after the forty days had ended. His encounter with the giant did not occur over a forty-day period at all. More examples could be given, but the point is clear: When examined in context, the scriptural support for Warren's formula is less than convincing.

We could also add some examples Warren did not use. For instance, Abraham learned patience while he waited for God's promised seed (Isaac)—a wait that lasted many years, not forty days (see Gen 21:2-3). Jacob learned humility, being forced to trust God, in one night while wrestling with an angel. This was preceded by fourteen years of working for Laban (Gen 32:24-30). Joseph was imprisoned for two full years before he was exalted to a high position in Egypt (Gen 41:1, 43). The apostle Paul's life was transformed in just a few minutes on the road to Damascus (Acts 9:1-9). And the list could go on and on.

Rather than teaching that "whenever God wanted to prepare someone for his purposes, he took 40 days," it is more accurate to say that sometimes God took 40 days, but not all the time, and not even most of the time. Rather, whenever God wanted to prepare someone for His purposes, He took however much time He deemed necessary to prepare that person. While a forty-day program might work as a helpful organizational tool, to claim that it is God's preferred method is far from accurate. That may seem a petty complaint to some, but Warren's overstatements about the significance of the forty days are all too typical of an increasingly popular, offhanded approach to Scripture that is devoid of proper care and accuracy (cf. 2 Tim 2:15; Jas 3:1).

2. An Incomplete Approach to Theology

In addition to an overly casual approach to Scripture, *The Purpose-Driven Life* also offers its readers an incomplete theological framework. This is somewhat surprising in an evangelical explanation of the overarching purpose of life. After all, in order for our purpose to truly be biblical, it should reflect the full extent of biblical teaching.

Yet, in spite of its broad premise, *The Purpose-Driven Life* seems theologically lopsided—downplaying certain themes in Scripture (such as God's wrath) while extensively emphasizing others (such as God's love). As a result, the importance of doctrine itself is minimized (see p. 34), while certain key areas of biblical teaching seem seriously shortchanged. For example, consider Warren's presentation of the gospel on pages 58-59:

> First, believe. Believe God loves you and made you for his purposes. Believe you're not an accident. Believe you were made to last forever. Believe God has chosen you to have a relationship with Jesus, who died on the cross for you. Believe that no matter what you've done, God wants to forgive you.

Second, receive. Receive Jesus into your life as your Lord and Savior. Receive his forgiveness for your sins. Receive his Spirit, who will give you the power to fulfill your life purpose. The Bible says, "Whoever accepts and trusts the Son gets in on everything, life complete and forever!" [John 3:36a] Wherever you are reading this, I invite you to bow your head and quietly whisper the prayer that will change your eternity: "Jesus, I believe in you and I receive you." Go ahead.

If you sincerely meant that prayer, congratulations! Welcome to the family of God! You are now ready to discover and start living God's purpose for your life.

To be sure, Warren's invitation includes several key aspects of the gospel. At the same time, it seems that other essential elements are missing. For example, repentance and self-denial are conspicuously absent (cf. Luke 9:23-24), as is a clear explanation of the eternal consequences of sin, or *why* Jesus died on the cross.[3] The fact that Warren waits to explain repentance until later in the book (under his teachings on spiritual growth, pp. 105, 182) almost hints at a pietistic (or "deeper life") perspective—where repentance and "surrendering to God" (see pp. 80-84) is wrongly viewed as separate, post-conversion experiences.[4]

Warren's definition of the "Good News" toward the end of the book (Day 37) hardly goes any deeper—emphasizing the benefits of grace without really explaining man's desperate condition. He states, "the Good News is that when we trust God's grace to save us through what Jesus did, our sins are forgiven, we get a purpose for living, and we are promised a future home in heaven" (p. 294). Yet, the rest of the chapter never explains the bad news—again leaving out a crucial part of the salvation message. In fairness, Warren does briefly mention hell (on pp. 37 and 112), but he does so almost in passing, without emphasizing the gravity of eternal condemnation.

The doctrine of God also seems to suffer in *The Purpose-Driven Life*. On the one hand, Warren rightly asserts, "We cannot just create our own comfortable or politically correct image of God and worship it. . . . To 'worship in truth' means to worship God as he is truly revealed in the Bible" (p. 101). On the other hand, the book seems to focus so much on God's love, kindness, and care that it simultaneously minimizes His less-"friendly" attributes (such as holiness, wrath, and judgment).

In the words of one reviewer:

> Warren continually tells us what God feels when we do certain things. He says, "Like a proud parent, God especially enjoys watching you use the talents and abilities he has given you" (Warren: 74). He also says, "You only bring him enjoyment by being you" (Warren: 75). Somehow Warren knows a cause and effect relationship between various things we do and God's emotions. He says, "God even enjoys watching you sleep!" (Warren: 75). He has discovered six secrets to being "a best friend of God" (Warren: 87).
>
> Warren's explanation of God leaves out many important truths and emphasizes those qualities that make God feel close and safe. This does not result in a full, biblical understanding of God. You will never hear about God's wrath against sin from Warren. You will never hear the warnings in the Bible about God's coming judgment. You will not learn about God's holiness from Warren. You will not hear passages like this: "See to it that you do not refuse Him who is speaking. For if those did not escape when they refused Him who warned them on earth, much less will we escape who turn away from Him who warns from heaven" (Hebrews 12:25).[5]

In other words, Warren's portrayal of God's nature is not complete. Yes, God is infinitely loving, caring, kind, and compassionate. But He is also perfectly holy, just, and righteous. By being unbalanced in his presentation of God's character, Warren does not fully represent who God is. And a right view of God is foundational to finding one's true purpose in life.

In other cases, the book borders on theological carelessness. At times, Warren's terminology sounds strikingly psychological. For example, his plan for overcoming sin includes "refocusing your thoughts" (p. 210), joining a "support group" (p. 212), and realizing "your vulnerability" (p. 215). In fact, patterns of sin (or "mistakes," p. 156) are reduced to "a repeating cycle of good intention-failure-guilt" in which people need "to be healed" because "you are only as *sick* as your secrets" (pp. 212-213, emphasis added). At other times the book presents non-evangelical figures as examples to be followed. Thus Benedictine monks (on p. 89) and Mother Teresa (on pp. 125 and 131), both representatives of Roman Catholicism, along with New Age leader Bernie Siegel (p. 31), are presented as positive role models. After all, these individuals are in step with the book's overall feel, where the emphasis is on love, community, and personal fulfillment. Doctrinal disagreements, on the other hand, take a backseat.

In contrast, the teaching of Christ and the apostles placed proper emphasis on the whole counsel of God—not just its more palatable parts. Jesus, for example, talked more about hell than heaven, demanded that unbelievers repent (Matt 4:17; Luke 5:32), insisted that believers take radical steps to deal with sin (Matt 5:29-30; 18:8-9), and argued that true discipleship may cost a person everything (Matt 10:32-39; Mark 8:34-38). Throughout the New Testament, the apostles echo these same themes (see Mark 6:12; Acts 2:38; 20:21; Heb 5:11-14), including the importance of doctrinal purity (Gal 1:6-10; Jas 3:17; Jude; 2 Pet 2). While Warren does not necessarily deny these themes, he does not seem to give them the weight and explanation that Scripture indicates they deserve—especially in a discussion on the overall purpose of life.

In view of such criticisms, Warren responds:

> I knew that by simplifying doctrine in a devotional format for the average person, I ran the risk of either understating or overstating some truths. I'm sure I have done that. I also knew that I'd be criticized for what I left out of the book and for using fifteen different translations and paraphrases to get the message across. But I decided when I planted Saddleback in 1980 that I'd rather reach large numbers of people for Christ than seek the approval of religious tradi-

tionalists. In the past eight years, we've baptized over 11,000 new adult believers at our church. I am addicted to changed lives.[6]

But is change that lacks doctrinal depth really biblical change? Scripture teaches that doctrine and duty go hand in hand. Proper living is always tied to proper thinking and proper theology. That's why, in so many of Paul's epistles, he spends the first part of the book teaching sound doctrine, and then the second half of the book discussing proper application.[7] Without a solid theological framework, Christians cannot have the biblical grid in place to live lives that are biblically sound.

3. An Inflated Position of Prominence

Third, it seems that some readers of *The Purpose-Driven Life* have promoted the book to a position of prominence that should only be reserved for Scripture. For example, one Amazon.com book reviewer put it this way:

> Our pastor asked us to replace our normal devotional with a 40-day study through "The Purpose-Driven Life." I'm not sure why we feel it's an okay thing to replace God's Word with a man's book, but I'm reading it any way.

Bob DeWaay, in his lengthy review, adds this:

> Rick Warren's eleven million copy bestseller has replaced Bible preaching in thousands of pulpits and has replaced the Bible in many thousands of Bible study groups. . . . The amazing thing is that thousands and thousands of groups around the world have taken Warren's advice ["I strongly urge you to gather a small group of friends and form a Purpose-Driven Life Reading Group to review these chapters on a weekly basis" (p. 307)] and began studying his book, leaving their Bibles at home. Pastors are preaching from Warren's materials rather than God's Word. Warren also says, "After you have gone through this book together as a group, you might consider studying other purpose-

driven life studies that are available for classes and groups" [p. 307]. The message of the gospel has been replaced with the method of Rick Warren. The Bible has been supplanted by the wisdom of man.[8]

Even a mainline Methodist church staff member agrees:

My church has jumped on what seems to be the latest church fad, *The Purpose-Driven Life* by Rick Warren. More than 70 members are enrolled in PDL classes. As a staff member I was strongly urged to take one. I'm just starting into the book, but it is setting off alarm bells for me. . . . In part [it's] the fact that people seem to be embracing it as if it were the Bible.[9]

Of course, we do not believe for a moment that Rick Warren really regards his own book that way, but it is hard to escape the force of the self-promoting language the book contains. For example, on page 11 Rick Warren says:

Because I know the benefits, I want to challenge you to stick with this spiritual journey for the next 40 days, not missing a single daily reading. Your life is worth taking the time to think about it. Make it a daily appointment on your schedule. If you will commit to this, let's sign a covenant together. There is something significant about signing your name to a commitment.

Readers are, in effect, encouraged to sign a formal vow to read it daily (cf. Jas 5:12; Matt 5:34-37; Deut 23:21-22); it's almost as though their personal devotions should revolve around *The Purpose-Driven Life*. To be sure, good Christian books can play a wonderful part in the believer's devotional life—as side dishes to the main course of Scripture. But when a book becomes a replacement for "the pure milk of the word" (1 Pet 2:1-2, NASB), whether in private devotions or in public sermons, something is not right.

Part of this problem may stem from the amazing promises that the book makes. From the very outset, *The Purpose-Driven Life* guarantees its readers that, if read and digested properly, the book (and forty-day program) will significantly change their lives for the better. On page 9 the author states:

> This is more than a book; it is a guide to a 40-day spiritual journey that will enable you to discover the answer to life's most important question: What on earth am I here for? By the end of this journey you will know God's purpose for your life and will understand the big picture—how all the pieces of your life fit together. Having this perspective will reduce your stress, simplify your decisions, increase your satisfaction, and, most important, prepare you for eternity.

Page 11 echoes this claim:

> As I wrote this book, I often prayed that you would experience the incredible sense of hope, energy, and joy that comes from discovering what God put you on this planet to do. There's nothing quite like it. I am excited because I know all the great things that are going to happen to you. They happened to me, and I have never been the same since I discovered the purpose of my life.

Quite clearly, *The Purpose-Driven Life* claims that it will not only inform its readers of their reason for existence but will also dramatically improve their current state of affairs. They will enjoy significant spiritual growth and life-change and will never again be the same, having been positively impacted by "all the great things" in store for them.

But are these promises realistic? In a sense the book seems to promise what only God can truly promise; it seems to suggest that a man-made book or program can do what only the Spirit of God can do. As a result, readers are set up for disappointment from the very beginning. Another Amazon.com reviewer said it this way:

> The back cover of this book states that it is a "groundbreaking manifesto on the meaning of life." The introduction states that

"this is more than a book; it is a guide to a 40-day spiritual journey that will enable you to discover the answer to life's most important question." This book did not live up to such a promise.

4. Its Seeker-Sensitive Family

Before concluding, one final concern must be raised. It is this: Because it is part of the Purpose-Driven family, *The Purpose-Driven Life* serves as an endorsement for other Rick Warren writings (specifically *The Purpose-Driven Church*), certain church programs (such as "The 40 days of Purpose Campaign"), and a broader evangelical phenomenon known as the seeker-sensitive movement.

While unpacking each of these related issues is not within the scope of this review, a few brief comments should be made:

The seeker-sensitive movement (which is encapsulated in *The Purpose-Driven Church*) emphasizes marketing techniques and business strategies as the primary method for healthy church growth.

As a result, seeker-sensitive churches tend to minimize the gospel message in order to soften topics such as sin, repentance, divine wrath, and eternal punishment. The goal is to make unbelievers feel comfortable until they are ready to accept Jesus. Hence, biblical sermons are often replaced with short talks, videos, and skits—anything that the audience will find more enjoyable and entertaining.

Success in the ministry is measured in terms of numbers of people in attendance. Whereas biblical success is defined as faithfulness to God, seeker-sensitive success is defined as a crowded building. Those who preach faithfully but never produce a large congregation (similar to the prophet Jeremiah) are told that they are doing something wrong.

By embracing *The Purpose-Driven Life*, some readers and churches may become unwittingly entangled in the seeker-sensitive movement—a philosophical system that is inherently unbiblical.[10]

CONCLUSION

Again we stress: *The Purpose-Driven Life* is not outright heresy. In fact, it highlights many biblical concepts, such as the importance of worship, fellowship, spiritual growth, spiritual service, and evangelism. That's why so many people love the book.

At the same time, its approach seems to be typical of contemporary evangelical trends—fluffy, feel-good, and watered-down. In our opinion, its treatment of Scripture is too casual, its doctrinal framework is too shallow, its self-made promises are too lofty, and its relationship to other market-driven products is too close to be ignored. Thus, in light of its shortcomings, we believe *The Purpose-Driven Life* should be read discerningly.

THE OLD PERƧPECTIVE ON PAUL: A CRITICAL INTRODUCTION TO
What Ƨaint Paul Really Ƨaid[1]

Phil Johnson

This chapter is adapted from a seminar given at The Metropolitan Tabernacle in London, England, in January 2004. It provides an introduction to the so-called "New Perspective on Paul." The New Perspective is a currently popular approach to understanding the New Testament, and its influence is quickly moving from the academic realm to evangelical pulpits. It usually involves significant modifications to the Protestant understanding of the doctrine of justification by faith. N. T. Wright's popular book, What Saint Paul Really Said, *is probably the most influential and simplest introduction to the major ideas of the New Perspective. While not intended as a complete analysis of every aspect of New Perspective teachings, this chapter serves as an introduction and critique for pastors and laypeople alike.*

At the moment several intense and important debates are stirring controversy among Reformed and evangelical leaders, all more or less centering on a new interpretive approach to the New Testament known as "The New Perspective on Paul." The debate is not merely an academic quarrel over unimportant hermeneutical nuances; it involves some real and significant threats to the doctrine Martin Luther called "the article by which the church stands or falls"—the doctrine of justification by faith. If the New Perspective is the correct perspective of Paul's teaching and theology, the Reformers were wrong on the main issue of the Reformation. Understandably, the New Perspective is sending shock waves of controversy into circles where Reformation principles are still deemed crucial biblical and theological distinctives.

The expression "New Perspective on Paul" was coined by James Dunn in a 1982 lecture describing this new approach to Pauline teaching that had roots going back to Albert Schweitzer in the early twentieth century and Lutheran theologian Krister Stendahl after the end of World War II. But the most important foundation for the New Perspective was a 1977 work of E. P. Sanders entitled *Paul and Palestinian Judaism*. Sanders rocked the academic world of contemporary Pauline studies with the revolutionary suggestion that the Judaism of Paul's day was not the self-righteous, works-based system that had been commonly assumed. James D. G. Dunn refined Sanders's views and added some twists of his own. None of those men were evangelicals, nor did they claim to be.

N. T. Wright, an Anglican archbishop and respected scholar, who is much closer to mainstream evangelicalism, has led the way among evangelicals who are adopting, adapting, and popularizing elements of these earlier authors (especially Dunn and Sanders). But Sanders, Wright, and Dunn also disagree among themselves on major points. So the New Perspective at the moment lacks the cohesiveness of a movement, and many observers have noted that there is not one monolithic "New Perspective on Paul," though many new perspectives share some common ideas and intersect with one another at key points.

THE BAſIC PREMIſE OF NEW PERſPECTIVE THEOLOGY

One thing virtually all advocates of the New Perspective do agree on, however, is that the historic Reformed understanding of Pauline soteriology (especially the Protestant understanding of justification by faith) is fundamentally flawed. In a nutshell, they suggest that the apostle Paul has been seriously misunderstood, at least since the time of Augustine and the Pelagian controversy, but even more since the time of Luther and the Protestant Reformation. They agree with Sanders's assertion that first-century Judaism has also been misinterpreted and misconstrued by New Testament scholars for hundreds of years, and therefore they believe the church's understanding of what Paul was teaching in Romans and Galatians has been seriously inaccurate at least since the time of Augustine.

Here are four important ways they say Paul has been misunderstood:

1. They Claim Paul Was Not Fighting Legalism

First, regarding first-century Judaism, keep in mind that the New Perspective on Paul starts with the claim that the Judaism of Paul's day was not really, after all, a religion of self-righteousness where salvation hinged on human works and human merit. So, according to this view, most New Testament scholars have utterly misunderstood Paul because they have misconstrued what he was up against. Even the Pharisees weren't legalists after all, it turns out. According to the New Perspective, the Jewish leaders of Paul's time have been misunderstood for centuries by biased exegetes who have erred because they have superimposed Augustine's conflict with Pelagius, as well as Luther's conflict with Roman Catholicism, onto their reading of Paul's conflict with the Judaizers.

Instead, according to the New Perspective, there was a strong emphasis on divine grace in the Judaism of Paul's time, and the Pharisees were not *really* guilty of teaching salvation by human merit. That is the one basic point upon which Sanders, Dunn, and Wright are all in full agreement. They base that claim primarily on their study of extrabiblical rabbinical sources, and they treat the matter as if it were settled in the world of New Testament scholarship—even though there are still plenty of weighty New Testament scholars who would strongly disagree with them. But that's the starting point of their view: First-century Judaism was not legalistic after all. For centuries, Christians have simply misunderstood what the Pharisees taught.

2. They See Racial Reconciliation as Paul's Primary Emphasis

Second, regarding the apostle Paul, the New Perspectivists are very keen to absolve Paul from the charge of anti-Semitism—and therefore they deny that he had any serious or significant *theological* disagreement with the Jewish leaders of his time. Obviously, if the religion of the Pharisees was a religion of grace and not human merit, then Paul would have had no fundamental disagreement with them regarding the doctrine of salvation.

But Paul's real controversy with the Jewish leaders, we are told, had to do with the way they treated Gentiles. It was not any kind of soteriological conflict. The Judaizers and the Pharisees were racial and cultural bigots who wanted to exclude all Gentiles from their fellowship, and Paul was seeking racial harmony and diversity in the covenant community. So the only significant complaint Paul had with Judaism was the racial and cultural exclusivity of its leaders.

3. They Limit the Gospel to a Declaration of Victory

Third, regarding the message of Christianity, the New Perspective on Paul claims that the gospel is an announcement about the lordship of Christ, period. It is the declaration that Christ, through His death and resurrection, has been shown by God to be Lord of creation and King of the cosmos. We would agree that this truth is an essential *feature* of the New Testament Gospel, of course. But we would not agree with advocates of the New Perspective when they say the gospel is therefore not really a message about personal and individual redemption from the guilt and condemnation of sin.

To quote Tom Wright in *What Saint Paul Really Said*, "[The gospel] is not . . . a system of how people get saved" (p. 45). Later he writes, "The announcement of the gospel results in people being saved. . . . But 'the gospel' itself, strictly speaking, is the narrative proclamation of King Jesus." "[The gospel is] the announcement of a royal victory" (p. 47). Ultimately, the New Perspective downplays or divests the gospel of every significant aspect of soteriology. The means of atonement is left vague in this system; the issues of personal sin and guilt are passed over and brushed aside. The gospel becomes nothing more than a proclamation of victory. In other words, the gospel of the New Perspective is decidedly *not* a message about how sinners can escape the wrath of God. In fact, this gospel says little or nothing about personal sin and forgiveness, individual redemption, atonement, or any of the other great soteriological doctrines. Soteriology is hardly a concern of the New Perspective, even when it comes to the gospel message.

4. They Redefine Justification by Faith

A *fourth* characteristic of the New Perspective is its unusual way of interpreting the Pauline doctrine of justification by faith and the Reformation principle of *sola fide*. Again, the New Perspective claims that historic Protestant Christianity has seriously confused and distorted what the apostle Paul taught about justification by faith. According to the New Perspective, when Paul wrote about *justification*, his concerns were (once again) corporate, national, racial, and social—not individual and soteriological.

According to those who advocate the new view, the doctrine of justification as taught by the apostle Paul has very little to do with personal and individual salvation from sin and guilt. Justification, they say, doesn't really pertain to *soteriology*, or the doctrine of salvation. It fits more properly in the category of *ecclesiology*, or the doctrine of the church.

To quote Tom Wright again, "What Paul means by justification . . . is not 'how you become a Christian,' so much as 'how you can tell who is a member of the covenant family'" (p. 122). On page 119, he says,

> "Justification" in the first century was not about how someone might establish a relationship with God. It was about God's eschatological definition, both future and present, of who was, in fact,

a member of his people. In Sanders' terms, it was not so much about "getting in," or indeed about "staying in," as about "how you could tell who was in." In standard Christian theological language, it wasn't so much about soteriology as about ecclesiology; not so much about salvation as about the church.

Again, and at every opportunity, the emphasis on personal and individual salvation is minimized or denied. The gospel is not really a message about redemption from sin and personal guilt; it is simply and only the declaration that Jesus is now Lord over all. Justification is not mainly about sin and forgiveness; it's about membership in the covenant community. And when you're done reading everything that has been written to promote the New Perspective, the issues of personal guilt, individual redemption, and atonement for sin have hardly been dealt with at all. All those weighty soteriological issues are left in a fog of uncertainty and confusion.

This redefinition of the doctrine of justification by faith is surely the greatest and most immediate danger posed by the New Perspective on Paul.[2] With that in mind, the rest of this chapter will address *this specific claim* that the doctrine of justification, in Paul's theology, is all about the Gentiles' standing in the covenant community rather than about the individual's standing before God as it relates to sin and forgiveness.

Without question, that is a total redefinition of justification—and one that, realistically speaking, is utterly impossible to harmonize with the historic Protestant understanding of justification by faith.

Certainly, the most conservative defenders of N. T. Wright and the New Perspective often insist that they *do* affirm what the great Protestant creeds teach regarding justification, and some of them have taken great pains to try to find language in the Westminster standards and other creeds that they can interpret as an affirmation of their views. But having read several such treatments and having dialogued at length with several devotees of the New Perspective who insist they are "Reformed," it is our conviction that when they are finished trying to reconcile their views with the historic evangelical and

Protestant view of justification by faith, all the main issues are left confused and muddled rather than clarified. That's because the New Perspective's view of justification is radically and fundamentally *different* from the classic view of justification by faith alone—which has always been understood as the central distinctive of every branch of historic Protestant Christianity.

N. T. WRIGHT AND JUSTIFICATION BY FAITH

In order to deal with such a large issue in the space allotted, the remainder of this chapter will focus on a just few of the most troubling statements made by Tom Wright in his book *What Saint Paul Really Said*. As a lay-level treatment of Wright's beliefs, *What Saint Paul Really Said* is certainly not as thorough and perhaps not as precise as his more academic works. On the other hand, since this work is a popular distillation of his perspective on the apostle Paul, aimed at serious laypeople and pastors, his aim ought to have been to convey his thoughts with the clearest, most concise, and most unambiguous language. This book is supposed to be a non-academic introduction to the New Perspective and a simple digest of the New Perspective's most important ideas. Thus, it deserves to be responded to on that basis—in a non-academic fashion, trying to deal with the big ideas and not getting bogged down in side issues and technicalities.

This chapter is therefore not intended to be a full, careful academic reply to Wright. Instead, it is designed to be a brief summary of why Wright's New Perspective is problematic, pointing out the major things to be on guard against in his work. As the subtitle suggests, this chapter is only a critical *introduction* to Wright's position.

No doctrine is more important in Protestant theology than the doctrine of justification by faith. This was the material principle of the Reformation, the central issue over which Rome and the Reformers fought and ultimately split. Calvin called justification by faith the principal hinge of all religion. But if Tom Wright and his New Perspective are correct, Luther and Calvin—and indeed *all* the Reformers—badly misunderstood the apostle Paul and seriously misconstrued the doctrine of justification. They were mistaken on the *main* issue. That is a very serious charge, but it is precisely what the New Perspective suggests.

(A corollary is that the scholars proposing this New Perspective are also claiming that they are the first people since the early church fathers who have correctly understood the Pauline epistles. That's an extremely bold stance to take—especially since it's a view that depends to such a large degree on the work of E. P. Sanders, who doesn't even accept the Pauline authorship of most of Paul's epistles.)

In *What Saint Paul Really Said*, Wright includes a chapter titled "Justification and the Church," in which he says that the traditional Protestant doctrine of justification "owes a good deal both to the controversy between Pelagius and Augustine in the early fifth century and to that between Erasmus and Luther in the early sixteenth century" (p. 113). But (according to Wright) the historic Protestant view of justification "does not do justice to the richness and precision of Paul's doctrine, and indeed distorts it at various points" (p. 113).

Notice that Wright is expressly arguing *against* a Reformed understanding of justification, and he repeatedly insinuates that Protestants need to rethink the whole doctrine and retool their teaching in light of *his* new understanding of what Paul really meant. On page 117, he claims that the classic Protestant understanding of justification has resulted in a reading of Romans that "has systematically done violence to that text for hundreds of years, and . . . it is time for the text itself to be heard again."

But Wright's own doctrine of justification is seriously deficient. In fact, he is at odds with Scripture on at least four major points related to this one issue of justification.

HIſ DEFINITION OF JUſTIFICATION

We've already seen a basic description of how Wright portrays the doctrine of justification. But here's how he himself states it in *What Saint Paul Really Said*, page 115: "The discussions of justification in much of the history of the church, certainly since Augustine, got off on the wrong foot—at least in terms of understanding Paul—and they have stayed there ever since." On page 120, he adds this:

> Despite a long tradition to the contrary, the problem Paul addresses in Galatians is not the question of how precisely someone becomes a Christian or attains to a relationship with God. (I'm not even sure how Paul would express, in Greek, the notion of 'relationship with God', but we'll leave that aside.) The problem he addresses is: should ex-pagan converts be circumcised or not? Now this question is by no means obviously to do with the questions faced by Augustine and Pelagius, or by Luther and Erasmus. On anyone's reading, but especially within its first-century context, [the problem] has to do, quite obviously, with the question of how you define the people of God. Are they to be defined by the badges of the Jewish race, or in some other way?

And so he concludes, "Justification, in Galatians, is the doctrine which insists that all who share faith in Christ belong at the same table, no matter what their racial differences, as they together wait for the final new creation" (p. 122).

In other words, according to Wright, justification is more a corporate issue than a personal one; it has more to do with the identity of the church than with the standing of the individual before God.

When Wright *does* connect the doctrine of justification with the individual's standing before God, it is nearly always in contexts where he is speaking of "final justification," which takes place in the eschatological future, at the last judgment, when God will judge men and women according to their *works.* In an article he has posted on the Internet titled "The Shape of Justification," Wright refers to "future justification" and cites Romans 2:13 as a proof text ("it is not the hearers of the law who are righteous before God, but the doers of the law who will be justified"). Thus Wright and other New Perspective writers seriously confuse the question of whether our standing as believers before God depends in some part on our own works, or whether Christ's work on our behalf is the sole and sufficient ground of our justification.

The way Wright speaks of this "future dimension" of justification is both careless and unclear. While in places he strenuously denies that justification is a process, he nonetheless believes that the individual Christian's standing before God is not truly settled until the final judgment, and then it will depend (at least in part) on the believer's own righteous works. That is almost precisely the point over which Rome and the Reformers fought their most important battles. If Wright is not on the Roman Catholic side of that issue, he certainly is *not* on the Reformers' side.

(On a side note, in that same online article, Wright insists that the doctrine of justification by faith is "a second-order doctrine," not an essential doctrine of Christianity. But the text of Galatians—and especially the anathema of Galatians 1:8-9—clearly indicates that the doctrine of justification is of primary importance. All the classic Reformed and Protestant creeds certainly treated justification as a first-order doctrine—if not the most important of all doctrines related to the gospel.)

HIS DESCRIPTION OF "WORKS OF THE LAW"

A second problem with Wright's teaching on justification involves his understanding of the phrase, "works of the law." Galatians 2:16 uses that expression three times in a single verse. "We know that a person is not justified by works of the law but through faith in Jesus Christ, so we also have believed in Christ Jesus, in order to be justified by faith in Christ and not by works of the law, because by works of the law no one will be justified." There are three other references to "works of the law" in Galatians (3:2, 5, 10) and one in Romans 9:32, and in each case the apostle Paul's point is the same: Legal obedience has no saving efficacy. Galatians 3:10 states: "all who rely on works of the law are under a curse."

Of course, the historic Protestant position has been that these very texts prove that Paul was saying the law condemns sinners and therefore our own efforts to obey the law cannot save us. Meritorious works of any kind are antithetical to grace. That is precisely what Paul states in Romans 11:6: "if it is by grace, it is no longer on the basis of works; otherwise grace would no longer be grace."

But Tom Wright says we need a new understanding of what Paul meant when he spoke of the works of the law. In his paper "The Shape of Justification," he defines "the works of the law" as "the badges of Jewish law-observance." He says Paul is speaking of circumcision, the dietary laws, and the priesthood—only the *ceremonial* aspects of Moses' law.

He is echoing Dunn, who wrote:

> "Works of the law" are nowhere understood here, either by his Jewish interlocutors or by Paul himself, as works which earn God's favor, as merit-amassing observances. They are rather seen as badges: they are simply what membership of the covenant people involves, what mark out the Jews as God's people. [What Paul denies in Galatians 2:16 is that] God's grace extends only to those who wear the badge of the covenant.

In other words, according to Wright and Dunn, Paul *isn't* saying that meritorious works in general contribute nothing to our justification. Rather, Paul's real point is that the distinctly Jewish elements of Moses' law don't guarantee covenant membership, and they cannot be used to exclude Gentiles from covenant membership. Or to put it more concisely, they are suggesting that Galatians 2:16 and biblical texts like it are *not* intended to deny that meritorious human works have any role whatsoever in justification.

Remember, according to Wright, this means that "justification, in Galatians, is the doctrine which insists that all who share faith in Christ belong at the same table, no matter what their racial differences" (p. 122). Again, Paul is not arguing against meritorious works; he is arguing against racial exclusivity.

Notice carefully: Wright at this point is not explicitly arguing that a person's works *do* provide grounds for his righteous standing before God; he is merely arguing that the standard proof-texts against such a doctrine prove no such thing. And so once again he stands against the Reformers and on the Roman Catholic side of the justification debate. At the very least, he leaves the door open for human merit as part of the grounds for our "final justification."

HIS DISTORTION OF "THE RIGHTEOUSNESS OF GOD"

Third, Wright misunderstands Paul's view of "the righteousness of God." This is a huge issue in *What Saint Paul Really Said*, deserving a more full treatment than it can be given here. But it must be mentioned.

Wright has a major section discussing the meaning of the phrase "the righteousness of God," beginning on page 95. In summary, he says that Protestants have always misunderstood the concept of divine righteousness. God's righteousness is His "covenant faithfulness." It is *not* "something that 'counts before' God or 'avails with' God" (p. 102). It's not something God can either impart or impute to sinners. When Scripture speaks of God's "righteousness," it's using the expression as a synonym for His covenant faithfulness.

In fact, Wright is so hostile to the notion of righteousness as something that counts with God that he paraphrases the traditional concept of righteousness out of Philippians 3:9 completely. In the actual text, Paul says that his great hope as a Christian is to "be found in him, not having a righteousness of my own that comes from the law, but that which comes through faith in Christ, the righteousness from God that depends on faith." But according to Wright, Paul is *really* "saying, in effect: I, though possessing covenant membership according to the flesh, did not regard that covenant membership as something to exploit; I emptied myself, sharing the death of the Messiah; wherefore God has given me the membership that really counts, in which I too will share the glory of Christ" (p. 124). So the "righteousness" that justifies the believer has been reduced to "covenant membership."

HIS DENIAL OF IMPUTATION

Before concluding, there is one final aspect of Wright's position that must be noted. Over and over again Tom Wright assaults the classic

Reformed doctrine that the righteousness of Christ is imputed, or reckoned, to the sinner's account and that it is on the ground of Christ's righteousness alone that we obtain our righteous standing before God.

Wright says that's nonsense. On page 98 he writes, "If we use the language of the law court, it makes no sense whatsoever to say that the judge imputes, imparts, bequeaths, conveys or otherwise transfers his righteousness to either the plaintiff or the defendant. Righteousness is not an object, a substance or a gas which can be passed across the courtroom."

Writing against the historic Reformed doctrine of imputation, he continues, "If we leave the notion of 'righteousness' as a law-court metaphor only, as so many have done in the past, this gives the impression of a legal transaction, a cold piece of business, almost a trick of thought performed by a God who is logical and correct but hardly one we would want to worship."

Is this to say that Christians are wrong to worship a God who justifies the ungodly and who is both just and the justifier of the one who believes in Jesus (cf. Rom 3:26)? May it never be! While space does not allow a more complete discussion of this topic, it is clear that Wright has drifted far from historic Reformed doctrine.

RESPONDING TO WRIGHT

How should Christians respond to N. T. Wright's understanding of justification by faith? Here are four brief, simple, biblical arguments that weigh heavily against New Perspective teaching:

1. Scripture Should Inform Our Understanding of First-Century Judaism

Our understanding of Judaism in the apostle Paul's culture ought to come primarily from Scripture itself and not from the musings of twenty-first century scholars who themselves refuse to bow to the authority of Scripture. Tom Wright has erred by lending more credence to the scholarship of men like Sanders and Dunn than he does to the testimony of Scripture.

The parable about the Pharisee and the publican, for example, gives us one of the best clues about what Scripture really means when it speaks of justification. The parable describes the justification of an individual before God. Luke 18:9 says Jesus told that parable "to some who trusted in themselves that they were righteous, and treated others with contempt." The New Perspective claims that kind of self-righteousness wasn't really a problem with the Judaism of Paul's and Jesus' time. Scripture plainly states otherwise. In fact, if we allow the Gospel accounts to inform our understanding of the Pharisees' religion, rather than selling out to the scholarship of E. P. Sanders, we *must* come to the conclusion that the old perspective of first-century Pharisaism is the correct one.

2. Scripture Should Shape Our Understanding of Paul's Teachings

Second, our understanding of *Paul's* doctrine of justification ought to come from the text of Scripture and not from questionable scholarship about first-century rabbinical views. To cite just one text that is impossible to reconcile with the New Perspective, listen to Acts 13:38-39, where we have Luke's record of how Paul preached the gospel in Antioch. After mentioning the resurrection, Paul said, "Let it be known to you therefore, brothers, that through this man forgiveness of sins is proclaimed to you." Clearly, the gospel Paul proclaimed is about personal forgiveness after all. And notice how he equates the forgiveness of sins with the doctrine of justification: "by him everyone who believes is freed from everything from which you could not be freed by the law of Moses."

Romans 4:4-8 is another passage that, when understood correctly, demolishes N. T. Wright's New Perspective on justification. It likewise speaks of individual justification from the guilt of sin, and it rules out meritorious works of all kind, not merely obedience to the ceremonial badges of Jewish identity: "Now to the one who works, his wages are not counted as a gift but as his due. And to the one who does not work but trusts him who justifies the ungodly, his faith is counted as righteousness, just as David also speaks of the blessing of the one to whom God counts righteousness apart from works: 'Blessed are those whose lawless deeds are forgiven, and whose sins are covered; blessed is the man against whom the Lord will not count his sin.'"

3. Scripture Should Frame Our Understanding of the Gospel

Third, notice that in the book of Romans, Paul's starting point for the gospel is divine wrath (Rom 1:18), and Paul begins his systematic treatment of gospel truth with almost two full chapters on the problems of sin and guilt. It seems quite clear that Paul had a very different notion of the gospel and the doctrine of justification than N. T. Wright does.

Openly motivated by ecumenical desires, Wright is deliberately reinterpreting biblical language (such as these key passages in Romans) in order to minimize the differences between Protestants and Roman Catholics. While his tactics may be subtle, couched in evangelical language and clothed in scholarly form, his interpretations do more to cloud Paul's true meaning than to clarify it.

Along those same lines, Sidney Dyer sums it up this way:

> The most disturbing material in Wright's book is that which sets forth his view of justification. . . . His view of justification is an attack on the very heart of the gospel. Paul warned of the danger of preaching another gospel in Galatians 1:8, "But if we, or an angel from heaven, preach any other gospel to you than what we have preached, let him be accursed." Paul, by using the words "any *other* gospel" (emphasis added), shows that he is attacking all other forms of the gospel, including therefore a proto-Pelagianism in the book of Galatians. It is against the backdrop of this attack that the true doctrine of justification shines so brightly and clearly. An unbeliever stands guilty before God as a criminal charged with a capital offense. He can only escape the judgment he deserves by believing in Christ who lived a righteous life and died an atoning death for sinners. Men are not waiting to stand

before God as members of one of two disputing parties in a civil lawsuit who are hoping that God will find in their favor.[3]

4. Scripture Should Be the Final Arbiter of All Our Opinions

Fourth and finally, it is ironic that N. T. Wight and other proponents of the New Perspective invariably complain that Luther and the Reformers were guilty of reading a conflict from their own time back into the New Testament. Clearly, N. T. Wright and his colleagues are themselves guilty of reading popular notions of twenty-first-century political correctness back into the text of the Pauline epistles. And the view they have come up with has a distinct post-modern slant. It is a perfect postmodern blend of inclusivism, anti-individualism, a subtle attack on certainty and assurance, and above all, ecumenism.

What they are really suggesting is that the apostle Paul was driven more by social and ecumenical concerns than by a concern for the standing of sinners before God. The New Perspective on Paul is, at the end of the day, an ecumenical, not an evangelical, movement.

Wright is totally frank about his ecumenical motives. Near the end of the book, on page 158, he writes:

> Paul's doctrine of justification by faith impels the churches, in their current fragmented state, into the ecumenical task. It cannot be right that the very doctrine which declares that all who believe in Jesus belong at the same table (Galatians 2) should be used as a way of saying that some, who define the doctrine of justification differently, belong at a different table. The doctrine of justification, in other words, is not merely a doctrine which Catholic and Protestant might just be able to agree on, as a result of hard ecumenical endeavour. It is itself the ecumenical doctrine, the doctrine that rebukes all our petty and often culture-bound church groupings, and which declares that all who believe in Jesus belong together in the one family. . . . The doctrine of justification is in fact the great *ecumenical* doctrine.

He goes on to add, moreover, that those of us who regard justification as central to the debate between Protestants and Catholics "have turned the doctrine into its opposite."

Frankly, we're happy to stand with Augustine and Luther and the rest of the Protestant Reformers—and with the Old-Perspective apostle Paul—against doctrine that weakens the very heart of the gospel. It is both surprising and saddening to see a novelty like this seducing so many men who profess to be Reformed in their theology. In reality, the New Perspective on Paul does not build on the advances of the Protestant Reformation. Rather it aims at destroying the Reformation at its very foundation. Put another way,

> Wright's view of justification is an attempt to reverse the Reformation. We must resist such attempts. The issue is one of life and death—eternal life and eternal death. When theological professors and pastors abandon the biblical and confessional doctrine of justification, they sacrifice the gospel and the souls of men.[4]

5

ROAMING WILD: INVEJTIGATING THE MEJJAGE OF
Wild at Heart[1]

Daniel Gillespie

If sales mean anything, the latest must-read book for men is John Eldredge's Wild at Heart—*a work in which the author showcases his definition of true masculinity. As a best-seller, the book's success underscores the importance of this topic in today's church, where Christian men are desperately searching for a biblical model to follow. Does* Wild at Heart *provide that model for them? To be sure, Eldredge cites Bible verses, references biblical characters, and highlights several of God's divine attributes. But are his ideas about biblical masculinity actually biblical? Or are they more firmly founded in his own extrabiblical experience? We'll consider those questions as we examine* Wild at Heart *by the light of Scripture.*

The Marines are looking for a few good men. But you won't find them in the church, says John Eldredge, at least not without some serious change.

In his best-selling book *Wild at Heart*, Eldredge examines the absence of biblical masculinity in contemporary Christianity, arguing that men must return to the rugged leaders they were designed to be. Even a cursory glance at modern society confirms Eldredge's bleak assessment and provokes the question, where did all the good men go? From the boardroom to the bedroom, from the ball field to the backyard, the absence of godly men has had a devastating impact on our culture.

The solution, according to Eldredge, is for Christian men to discover true masculinity—something they can do only in the wilderness. After all, men are not really at home in an office or a taxicab. Nor are they alive on a downtown sidewalk. Instead, men belong to the frontiers, where they will find a battle to fight, a beauty to rescue, and an adventure to live. Real men need adventure, danger, and physical challenge to be fulfilled. That's why so many men are bored in American churches and dissatisfied with spiritual pursuits. Clearly, they cannot discover their God-given purpose in our modern urban society. Instead, they must find their hearts "out there on the burning desert sands" (p. 6).

Armed with an engaging writing style and a timely appeal, Eldredge's message has certainly struck a chord with Christian men around the globe. In fact, since its publication the book has sold more than a million copies—giving its author one of the most influential voices on the topic to date. Many churches, Bible studies, and small groups have embraced the book as a groundbreaking perspective on true masculinity. And the book has also been endorsed by high-profile evangelical leaders. For example, Pastor Chuck Swindoll, in the foreword to *Wild at Heart*, calls the book "excellent," full of "splendid ideas," and "the best, most insightful book I have read in the last five years."

But are such accolades really justified? Does John Eldredge truly present men with the means to manhood? Certainly the author has identified a clear problem. But has he diagnosed the cure correctly? Or is he actually leading Christian men further away from where God wants them to be?

We believe a thorough assessment of *Wild at Heart* reveals that Eldredge's solution, although innovative, falls far short of true masculinity. In fact, many of Eldredge's arguments are directly opposed to the biblical teaching on the subject. This chapter will highlight four critical categories where *Wild at Heart* roams off the biblical path.

AN INSUFFICIENT VIEW OF SCRIPTURE

Foundational to each of the flaws in *Wild at Heart* is an insufficient view of Scripture. Whether it is an absence of biblical support or a severely misapplied text, Eldredge wields the sword of truth clumsily in a faltering attempt to make his book Christian.

From the first chapter to the last, Eldredge never is clear about where his ultimate authority lies. On the one hand, he quotes Scripture and uses biblical examples to support his position. But on the other, he references movies, poems, books, and other authors as if they were equal to, if not weightier than, God's Word. On page 200, he says:

> God is intimately personal with us and he speaks in ways that are peculiar to our own hearts—not just through the Bible, but through the whole of creation. To Stasi he speaks through movies. To Craig he speaks through rock and roll (he called me the other day after listening to "Running Through the Jungle" to say that he was fired up to go study the Bible). God's word to me comes in many ways—through sunsets and friends and films and music and wilderness and books.

An overemphasis on Hollywood. If asked, Eldredge would probably agree that Scripture must be the final authority in a believer's life. Unfortunately, his book suggests otherwise. With more than sixty references to films and movie characters, Eldredge inundates his readers with Hollywood's portrait of masculinity. In the words of one reviewer,

> We read about *Legends of the Fall, Braveheart, Gladiator, A River Runs Through It, Saving Private Ryan, Bridge on the River Kwai, The Magnificent Seven, Shane, Top Gun, Die Hard, Flying Tigers,* and *The*

Natural. One quickly finds that it is Eldredge's film background, not his biblical expertise, that forms the primary source for his conclusions.[2]

To be fair, Eldredge's examples often picture a man of integrity, fortitude, and passion, all of which are important traits for biblical manhood. But his sources and the authority for his claims are still inherently questionable. Is Hollywood where Christians should go to find out what God expects for men? Should movies form the foundation, or furnish the role models, for true masculinity? Since when does the church develop its spiritual ideals from the on-screen imaginations of unsaved directors? At the very least, Eldredge (who graduated from college with a theater degree) sends a confusing message to his audience—especially when the film characters he spotlights often exemplify less than biblical behavior and values.

Listen to what Eldredge says on page 13: "Compare your experience watching the latest James Bond or Indiana Jones thriller with, say, going to Bible study." In other words, when compared to adrenaline-packed blockbusters, Eldredge seems to suggest that God's Word loses out. But should spiritual endeavors even be compared to special effects? Should the Bible be rated in terms of its entertainment value? Of course not. Certainly, Eldredge's desire to see thrill, excitement, and energy infused into the Christian experience is a good one. Unfortunately, in searching for renewed spiritual passion, Eldredge begins with the film industry rather than primarily looking to the Scriptures.

An overemphasis on other extrabiblical sources. The author's extrabiblical support does not end with Hollywood. Quotes from secular song writers, poets, and philosophers also line the pages of *Wild at Heart.* From the Dixie Chicks to the Eagles to Bruce Springsteen, Eldredge seems enamored by the thoughts of worldly men. He quotes Robert Bly, a self-proclaimed student of Sigmund Freud, more than twenty times in this book. It is as if Eldredge is making a deliberate attempt to use secular sources in order to seem relevant. Again, this preoccupation with "relevance" results in the elevation of contemporary human wisdom, while orthodox biblical teaching takes a conspicuous backseat.

Eldredge's reliance on extrabiblical sources is most striking when he recounts the supposed revelations he's received from God. On page 103 Eldredge writes, "I heard Jesus whisper a question to me: 'Will you let me initiate you?' Before my mind ever had a chance to process, dissect and doubt the whole exchange, my heart leaped up and said yes." Without thinking or examining Scripture, he responds to what he thinks to be the voice of God. But how does he know this is from God? Eldredge later admits that sometimes such voices may not have God as their source. On page 134 he says, "You must ask God what he thinks of you, and you must stay with the question until you have an answer.... This is the last thing the Evil One wants you to know. He will play the ventriloquist; he'll whisper to you as if he were the voice of God."

Yet Eldredge himself seems to showcase the revelations he's received without any caution whatsoever. For example, on page 135 Eldredge recounts an alleged conversation (in the form of a journal entry) that he had with God.

> What of me, dear Lord? Are you pleased? What did you see? I am sorry that I have to ask, wishing I knew without asking. Fear, I suppose, makes me doubt. Still, I yearn to hear from you—a word, or image, a name or even just a glance from you.
>
> This is what I heard:
> *You are Henry V after Agincourt . . . the man in the arena, whose face is covered with blood and sweat and dust, who strove valiantly . . . a great warrior . . . yes, even Maximus.* And then *You are my friend.*

But how can he be confident that this is the Lord? Maybe it's actually a sly deception from Satan or the workings of an overactive imagination. Whatever the case, it's hard to envision the Lord of the universe resorting to movies to reveal spiritual truth.

Eldredge continues, on page 135, to describe how he felt after the interaction:

I cannot tell you how much those words mean to me. In fact, I'm
embarrassed to tell them to you; they seem arrogant. . . . They are
words of life, words that heal my wound and shatter the Enemy's
accusations. I am grateful for them, deeply grateful.

It's remarkable how different these words are from those of men like
David (see Ps 19) and Paul (see 2 Tim 3:16-17) who reserved such
praise for the written Word of God alone. Whether intended or not,
Eldredge continually elevates his own thoughts (which he attributes
to God) above the written Word (once for all delivered to the saints;
cf. Jude 3). Such flippancy is dangerous, especially since the
Scriptures reserve severe warnings for this kind of presumption (see
Rev 22:18-19).

A de-emphasis on key biblical texts. Eldredge's abundant use of non-
biblical support provides a stark contrast to his noticeable absence of
key biblical texts on manhood. Sure, Eldredge calls attention to some
specific verses that describe God as a warrior or demonstrate Christ's
zeal. But in a book specifically targeted at Christian men, how could
he overlook texts such as Ephesians 5:25-33 and Titus 2:1-8? These
are passages where men are given explicit commands and the essence
of biblical masculinity is directly addressed. In an effort to be relevant
and fresh, Eldredge has left the believer's most effective tool on the
shelf. In so doing, he ends up contradicting much of what Scripture
actually teaches about manhood.

It is likely that these texts were overlooked because, generally
speaking, they contradict the entire thesis of Eldredge's book. For
example, in Titus 2:2 older men are called "to be sober-minded, dignified, self-controlled, sound in faith, in love, and in steadfastness."
Four verses later the young men are commanded "to be self-controlled. Show yourself in all respects to be a model of good works, and
in your teaching show integrity, dignity, and sound speech that cannot be condemned." This is a far cry from the wild, unfettered,
adventure-seeking movie star who is uncritically made the hero in
Wild at Heart.

An inaccurate method of biblical interpretation. When Scripture *is* incorporated into *Wild at Heart*, it is often out of context or poorly balanced with the full canon of God's Word. In examining Old Testament saints Eldredge makes a common but harmful error in biblical study. He assumes that there is no distinction between prescriptive and descriptive texts in the Bible. By doing this, he confuses events, descriptions, and characteristics highlighted in narrative passages with direct commands given to the New Testament believer. Consider his comments on page 5:

> Look at the heroes of the biblical text: Moses does not encounter the living God at the mall. He finds him (or is found by him) somewhere out in the deserts of Sinai, a long way from the comforts of Egypt. The same is true of Jacob, who has his wrestling match with God not on the living room sofa but in a wadi somewhere east of the Jabbok, in Mesopotamia. Where did the great prophet Elijah go to recover his strength? To the wild. As did John the Baptist, and his cousin, Jesus, who is *led by the Spirit* into the wilderness.

But do these few examples really show us that God *always* uses wilderness experiences to change men's lives? Of course not. Scripture speaks highly of many men who "encountered God" without losing themselves in nature. Take Joseph (in an Egyptian prison), for example, or Daniel (in a Babylonian palace), or Nehemiah (in a Medo-Persian royal court), or the apostle Paul (on the road to Damascus). These are just a few examples of men whom God greatly impacted, even while they resided in urban areas. In direct contrast to Eldredge's premise, the overall message of the Bible makes it clear: God is not nearly as concerned with the location of your life as He is with the condition of your heart.

With so much of the Bible being narrative, almost any principle imaginable could be supported by confusing prescriptive and descriptive texts. For example, after reading the life of Elisha, someone might argue that being mauled by wild bears is a proper punishment for disrespectful children (see 2 Kings 2:23-25). Of course, such an interpretation would be outrageous. But the principle behind it is essentially no different than that found on page 5 of *Wild at Heart*.

Another example of careless Bible study is Eldredge's explanation of the book of Ruth. Throughout history, the vast majority of Bible scholars have understood the theme of the book to center on God's providence in extending the Messianic line. In contrast, Eldredge claims, "The book of Ruth is devoted to one question: How does a good woman help her man to play the man? The answer: She seduces him" (p. 191). This is certainly a novel interpretation—bordering on both the bizarre and the blasphemous.

Scripture makes it clear that the written Word of God alone contains everything we need for "life and godliness" (2 Pet 1:3; see also Ps 119:105 and 2 Tim 3:15-17). To set aside the Bible's truth in favor of worldly wisdom and film references is to treat it carelessly and scornfully. We must approach God's Word on His terms, not with our own agendas—simply looking for proof-texts for our own ideas. Yet, that is exactly how the Bible is used in *Wild at Heart*. And that is why, at the most foundational levels, Eldredge's arguments fall seriously short.

AN INADEQUATE PICTURE OF GOD

A second fundamental flaw in *Wild at Heart*, flowing from an insufficient view of Scripture, is an inadequate portrayal of who God is. While Eldredge attempts to support his thesis by appealing to God's character, he handicaps his readers by giving them less than the full story. Granted, in a short book with a specific theme it is impossible to include all that Scripture has to say about the Creator and Sustainer of the world. Nonetheless, the author's lack of balance is indefensible. Eldredge emphasizes only the divine attributes that give credence to his idea of masculinity. Other attributes are conveniently omitted.

For example, Eldredge argues that godly men should not necessarily be "nice guys." On page 25, he supports this premise by looking to the actions of God: "I wonder if the Egyptians who kept Israel under the whip would describe Yahweh as a Really Nice Guy?

Plagues, pestilence, the death of every firstborn—that doesn't seem very gentlemanly now does it?" Does this mean that godly men should also wreak havoc on their enemies? By emphasizing God's justice, wrath, and power, Eldredge certainly promotes God's authority. Yet, while he continually refers to God as a warrior, he fails to ever mention one of God's most awesome attributes—His mercy. And this is no minor oversight. Divine grace runs like a river through every page of Scripture from the Old Testament to the New. God is merciful, gracious, and kind. The entire plan of redemption is an act of unparalleled and unimaginable mercy; yet nowhere in *Wild at Heart* is this attribute discussed.

Eldredge continues this trend on page 29, where he conveniently highlights the virile and untamed aspects of God's creation: "If you have any doubts as to whether or not God loves wildness, spend a night in the woods . . . alone. Take a walk out in a thunderstorm. Go for a swim with a pod of killer whales. Get a bull moose mad at you." Again, God's power in the wilderness is unmistakable. But God's character and His glory are equally evident in the beauty of a sunset, the complexity of the human eye, and the gentleness of a newborn baby. Because Eldredge's premise demands that God also be "wild at heart," he fails to present the full array of divine character traits.

Wild at Heart not only shortchanges several of God's praiseworthy attributes, it also misconstrues others. One of the most significant examples of this involves God's sovereignty. On page 30, Eldredge argues:

> In an attempt to secure the sovereignty of God, theologians have overstated their case and left us with a chess-player God playing both sides of the board, making all his moves and all ours too. But clearly, this is not so. God is a person who takes immense risks.

Later on the same page, he continues by asking, "Does God cause a person to sin? 'Absolutely not!' says Paul (Gal 2:17). Then he can't be moving all the pieces on the board, because people sin all the time." And finally, on page 31, Eldredge contends that "He [God] did not *make* Adam and Eve obey him. He took a risk."

Once again, in an attempt to make God into an adventure-chasing thrill-seeker, Eldredge warps the biblical picture of God's sovereignty. Consider the following verses:

> *I know that you can do all things, and that no purpose of yours can be thwarted. (Job 42:2)*

> *Behold, I am the LORD, the God of all flesh. Is anything too hard for me? (Jer 32:27)*

> *The lot is cast into the lap, but its every decision is from the LORD. (Prov 16:33)*

> *I am the LORD; that is my name; my glory I give to no other, nor my praise to carved idols. Behold, the former things have come to pass, and new things I now declare; before they spring forth I tell you of them. (Isa 42:8-9)*

The God of the Bible is not a God who takes "risks." There are no unknowns with God. He has foreordained everything in history from before the foundation of the world (Eph 1). In fact, the book of Revelation makes it clear: God already knows how human history will end. It's certainly true that God is never the efficient cause or author of the evil that men do, but Scripture nonetheless teaches that He exercises His sovereignty even in the very worst acts of evil (Acts 2:23-24; 4:27-28). Nothing comes as a surprise to Him. His plan is comprehensive and eternal (Isa 45:21).

Unlike Hollywood's heroes, who take startling risks to save the day, the God of Scripture sits enthroned in heaven, confidently and calmly in control of all creation.

> *. . . for I am God, and there is no other; I am God, and there is none like me, declaring the end from the beginning and from ancient times things not yet done, saying, "My counsel shall stand, and I will accom-*

plish all my purpose," calling a bird of prey from the east, the man of
my counsel from a far country. I have spoken, and I will bring it to pass;
I have purposed, and I will do it. (Isa 46:9-11)

The Bible could not be more clear: There are no risks with God.
But Eldredge seems to have overlooked the biblical evidence. As a
result, he continually replaces Scripture's portrait of our sovereign
God with his own self-styled definition. For example, on page 12 he
describes God as "wild, dangerous, unfettered and free."

Granted, Eldredge does make a brief attempt to disassociate
himself from Open Theism. (Open Theism is a relatively new theological position that proposes that God is unsure about the future,
but He is trying His best to make it all work out in the end.) But the
author's defense is unconvincing. On page 32 he concedes that "we
must humbly acknowledge that there's a great deal of mystery
involved, but for those aware of the discussion, I am not advocating
open theism. Nevertheless, there is definitely something wild in the
heart of God."

This type of theological double-talk does not hold water.
According to *Wild at Heart*, God is a God of risk, and risk only exists
if the outcome is unsure. But this is certainly not the position of
orthodox Christianity, nor is it in keeping with the overall tenor of
Scripture. Denying the sovereignty of God is not only a blatant
affront to His Person but also an outright denial of His Word.

AN INCOMPLETE PORTRAIT OF CHRIST

Wild at Heart's haphazard handling of deity is not confined to the
heavenly Father alone. It is also seen in the book's depiction of Jesus
Christ. Correctly asserting that Jesus is a model for masculinity,
Eldredge fails by only giving half of the story.

Without question, there is no better model for masculinity than
Jesus Christ. As the Son of Man, the Bible depicts Him as the perfect
man—100 percent human and yet without sin. At the same time, as
the Son of God He is the supreme object of our faith and the fault-

less example we are to follow. As the apostle Paul told his readers in
1 Corinthians 11:1, "Be imitators of me, as I am of Christ."

Eldredge should certainly be applauded for seeking to present
Christ as a model for manhood. Nonetheless, he falls short when he
limits the characteristics of Christ to those that fit his thesis. The
image of Christ found in *Wild at Heart* is that of a man who cleansed
the temple, confronted the Pharisees, and never cowered in the face
of opposition. He describes Jesus on page 29, saying:

> Jesus is no "capon priest," no pale-faced altar boy with his hair
> parted in the middle, speaking softly, avoiding confrontation, who
> at last gets himself killed because he has no way out. He works
> with wood, commands the loyalty of dockworkers. He is the Lord
> of hosts, the captain of angel armies. And when Christ returns, he
> is at the head of a dreadful company, mounted on a white horse,
> with a double-edged sword, his robe dipped in blood (Rev. 19).
> Now that sounds a lot more like William Wallace than it does
> Mother Teresa. No question about it—there is something fierce
> in the heart of God.

But in Eldredge's portrayal of Christ, these macho characteristics
are never balanced by the true biblical descriptions of Christ's meekness, gentleness, and mercy. While it is true that Christians often mis-
represent Jesus as passive and effeminate, Eldredge has reacted by
swinging to the other extreme. Eldredge's Christ—a zealous radical
who always seems ready to fight—is an equally inaccurate portrayal
of the biblical Jesus.

One example of Eldredge's one-sided presentation is found on
page 151, where he says, "You must let your strength show up.
Remember Christ in the Garden, the sheer force of his presence?
Many of us have actually been afraid to let our strength show up
because the world doesn't have a place for it." Yet even in that passage, Eldredge misses the fact that Christ did *not* stand up for
Himself or attempt to fight back. In fact, he even reprimanded Peter
for acting like the hero of *Gladiator* and attempting to retaliate.

"Then Jesus said to him, 'Put your sword back into its place. For all who take the sword will perish by the sword'" (Matt 26:52). By conveniently overlooking this portion of the text, Eldredge distorts the entire passage.

On pages 78 and 79, while giving advice to one of his sons who had recently encountered a neighborhood bully, Eldredge says:

> "Blaine, look at me." He raised his tearful eyes slowly, reluctantly. There was shame written all over his face. "I want you to listen very closely to what I am about to say. The next time that bully pushes you down here is what I want you to do—are you listening, Blaine?" He nodded, his big wet eyes fixed on mine. "I want you to get up . . . *and I want you to hit him . . . as hard as you possibly can*" [emphasis added]. A look of embarrassed delight came over Blaine's face, then he smiled. . . .
>
> Yes, I know that Jesus told us to turn the other cheek. But we have really misused that verse. You cannot teach a boy to use his strength by stripping him of it. Jesus was able to retaliate, believe me. But he chose not to. And yet we suggest that a boy who is mocked, shamed before his fellows, stripped of all power and dignity should stay in that beaten place because Jesus wants him there? You will emasculate him for life.

Is this really what Jesus meant when He commanded us to turn the other cheek (Matt 5:39)? What about Christ's commands to "love your enemies and pray for those who persecute you" (Matt 5:44)? Again, Eldredge completely misrepresents God's Word, replacing Christ's clear instruction with his own worldly wisdom and advice.

Note that in attempting to teach his son strength and to defend his masculinity, Eldredge completely ignores Jesus' supreme example, as he himself says in passing: "Jesus was able to retaliate . . . but he chose not to." That *is* true strength despite Eldredge's self-styled conclusions. The ability to demonstrate grace under fire comes only from the work of the Spirit in the lives of believers. If biblical masculinity is measured in terms of fighting back, then what about the example of Jesus, which we are expressly commanded to follow? "When he was reviled, he did not revile in return; when he suffered, he did not threaten" (1 Pet 2:23). Jesus' example leaves us with only one possible conclusion—Eldredge is wrong to equate turning the other cheek with "weakness" (p.79).

Christ, of course, was the antithesis of weakness. But His power is seen more in his constant restraint than in His rare display of action. Yet Eldredge presents Christ as "fierce, wild and romantic to the core" (p. 203). That type of misrepresentation has lead some critics, such as Rut Ethridge III, to protest by saying:

> Is Christ wild? Since Christ is in absolute control of all things (Mark 4:39-41), the term "wild" just does not apply to Him. Further, when we examine the distinctive personhood of Christ and His Messianic role, we see not wildness, but pure and complete submission. Jesus said and did only what the Father wanted Him to (John 8:28-29; Philippians 2:7-8), and He lived in complete submission to the Law (Matthew 5:17-18). Our very salvation depended on Christ's lack of wildness! (Romans 5:18-19). Sure, Christ railed against Pharisaical hypocrisy and drove money changers from the temple, but are those things really indicative of wildness . . . or self-controlled, passionate obedience to the Father? How can the very personification of meekness, humility, and absolute power be considered wild?

To view Christ more like William Wallace than Mother Theresa, as Eldredge does on page 29, is not the issue. After all, Christ cannot ultimately be compared to anyone. Instead, the issue is our likeness to Christ. *He* is the standard, not William Wallace, John Wayne, or James Bond. Christ and Christ alone is the true standard for manhood and masculinity. This is seen in His person and life, and it is commanded in His Word. Yes, Christ demonstrated passion, leadership, and power. But He also showed great mercy, meekness, and self-control. Eldredge is right in turning to Christ, but he fails to present Jesus accurately—as both the sovereign King and the suffering Servant.

AN INACCURATE PORTRAIT OF MAN

A final flaw exhibited in *Wild at Heart* is an incorrect and unbiblical view of man—a flaw that is especially alarming in a book about finding true masculinity. Eldredge's misguided anthropology is seen in at least two ways.

Man's personal responsibility for sin is overlooked. Instead of establishing individual responsibility for sin, the author encourages men to shift the blame—seeing sin more as a sickness than a moral choice. An entire chapter (4) deals with the "wounds" that every man has—wounds that help explain who a man is and why he acts as he does. In other words, every man is a victim of some ill treatment: Either your father was too passive, or your father was too controlling; you were given too much responsibility or too much freedom. Either way everyone has a "wound." On page 127 he states, "There are readers who even now have no idea what their wound is, or even what false self arose from it. Ah, how convenient that blindness is. Blissful ignorance. But a wound unfelt is a wound unhealed."

By convincing his readers to blame their behavior on these hidden wounds, Eldredge replaces the guilt of a sinner with the self-righteous pity of a victim. That falls far short of the biblical picture of man's responsibility. The apostle Paul doesn't cry out for mercy based on his upbringing or his legalistic Jewish parents. Instead he proclaims, "The saying is trustworthy and deserving of full acceptance, that Christ Jesus came into the world to save sinners, of whom I am the foremost" (1 Tim 1:15). In Romans 3:23 he calls for everyone to recognize their sinful state: "For all have sinned and fall short of the glory of God." Despite his many hardships, Paul never complained of being victimized. He did not reject or deny his sin, nor did he excuse the sinfulness of others as a wound inflicted on them. Instead, Paul recognized the reality and subsequent responsibility of human depravity (cf. Ps 51:4-5).

Wild at Heart, on the other hand, downplays sin at every turn. By shifting the focus away from sin, Eldredge diminishes man's guilt before God and de-emphasizes his need for repentance. "Things began to change for Carl when he saw the whole sexual struggle not so much as sin *but as a battle for his strength*" (p. 147). Without embracing sin as man's true problem, the author badly misdiagnoses man's greatest need. Scripture makes it abundantly clear that God will hold each individual accountable for sin (Rom 3:23; 6:23). That is our real problem, and all of Scripture affirms this. And therefore our deepest need is for a Savior, not a healing hand or a further affirmation of our strength. The "wounds" Eldredge encourages men to hide behind may be popular, but they are not biblical.

Man's purpose in life is misconstrued. In addition to neglecting a proper view of sin, Eldredge also misunderstands God's purpose for men. This is not surprising since, instead of looking to God's Word for the answer, he looks instead to his own wants and desires. Thus, on page 48 he contends:

> Why does God create Adam? What is a man for? If you know what something is designed to do, then you know its purpose in life. A retriever loves the water; a lion loves the hunt; a hawk loves to soar. It's what they're made for. Desire reveals design, and design reveals destiny. In the case of human beings, our design is also revealed by our desires.

What is Eldredge saying? Put simply, man's purpose should be determined by his passions and pleasures. Because men have a desire for adventure, battles, and beauties, then that must be what they were designed to pursue. In assuming this, the author overlooks the fact that, as fallen human beings, our desires are inherently sinful and selfish. Moreover, he makes man's purpose in life self-centered instead of God-centered. Christ said that He came to do the will of the Father and not His own (see Luke 22:42). In contrast, Eldredge claims the key to biblical manhood starts with embracing our own wills above anything else.

In a bookstore years ago, Eldredge "ran across a sentence that changed [his] life." The sentence, from author Gil Bailie, was this: "Don't ask yourself what the world needs. Ask yourself what makes you come alive, and go do that, because what the world needs is people who have come alive" (p. 200). If this is Eldredge's life motto, it's no wonder he sees selfish ambition as the key to godly living. But this is certainly not in keeping with the instruction of Scripture (see Phil 2:1-4). Contrary to Eldredge's claims, what the world needs is selfless men who obey Christ and proclaim His gospel—seeking to serve Him rather than themselves. Christ calls us to deny ourselves and follow Him (Mark 8:34). It seems Eldredge is calling us to do just the opposite.

CONCLUSION

There is no question that *Wild at Heart* addresses a critical topic in Christianity. There is a serious need for men with resolve, strength, and character. However, by failing to establish a high view of Scripture, a high view of God, and a proper view of man, Eldredge lays a faulty foundation for constructing true masculinity. His call to be a wild man is not only unnecessary—it is unbiblical. Men are to be dignified and above reproach, not dangerous and beyond restraint. The man behind the desk can be just as much a man of God as the mighty warrior of the Old Testament—if he holds fast to what God's Word commands him to be (see Eph 5; Titus 2).

So let the man who searches for true masculinity look no further than the pages of Scripture, for there he will find the truth about himself from the mouth of his Creator. Let his ears not be tickled by the whims of men, but let his mind be trained by the Word of God. And before any man looks for his battle to fight, his beauty to rescue, and his adventure to live, let him first look to his God to glorify.

6

WHEN THE TRUTH BECOMEſ A TABLOID: A CLOſER LOOH AT
The Revolve New Teſtament[1]

Rick Holland

This chapter reminds us that discernment is needed not only on the bookshelf, but also on the magazine rack. With the popularity of secular teenage magazines such as YM *and* Seventeen, *it's little wonder that Christian publishers finally followed suit. In this case, Transit Books created* Revolve, *a glossy, magazine-style New Testament aimed at teenage girls. (Transit Books has also recently released* Refuel *for teenage boys, along with several other Bible-zines.) Filled with catchy call-outs and trendy pictures,* Revolve *certainly mimics the style and layout of other teenage periodicals. But have they been able to maintain the integrity of the New Testament at the same time? This chapter, originally published as an article for* Pulpit *magazine, separates the content from the cosmetics to reveal the true face of* Revolve.

The Bible has been reprocessed in postmodernity in a variety of ways. These include audio tapes with accompanying sound effects, cinematic and television productions with dramatic savvy and special effects, claymation enlivened with the voices of celebrities, comic books with colorful caricatures, computer-generated vegetables that talk and sing with astonishing biblical acumen, eschatological novels and movies, even Broadway musicals with amazing technicolor dreamcoats.

So it should surprise few that the Bible is undergoing yet another face-lift, this time under the creative scalpel of the editors of Transit Books, a division of Thomas Nelson, Inc. But like a recent photo of Michael Jackson, this latest makeover of the Holy Bible looks very little like the original.

Meet *Revolve*. It is an edition of the New Testament that uses as much camouflage as a Stealth B-2 bomber in its efforts to disguise itself. Looking nothing like any other Bible, *Revolve* was designed to spare teenage girls the embarrassment of being caught with a traditional copy of the Scriptures.

At first glance, *Revolve* looks like any other glossy teen magazine splashed with photos of attractive and trendy co-eds, colorful call-out boxes, and advertisements. This teen 'zine could sit on the shelf next to copies of *Glamour* and *YM* and appear to be just another pop-culture offering. But a closer look at the cover reveals four unexpected words cutting across the top: "The Complete New Testament."

The creators of *Revolve* wanted to design a Bible that looked at home in the backpacks of twelve- to seventeen-year-old girls. Laurie Whaley of Thomas Nelson said, "Teens were saying that they found the Bible to be too freaky, too big, too intimidating. . . . *Revolve* shows girls that reading the New Testament is just as easy as reading an issue of *Seventeen* or *Vogue*."[2]

Right alongside the text of the New Testament are call-out boxes like those found in any other teen magazine. These "bonus" features include Christian Q & A's, devotional thoughts, shopping tips, beauty secrets, opinions from guys, advertisements, top-ten lists, and quizzes. So, how do these supplements tie-in with Scripture?

Let me take you on a quick tour of *Revolve* . . .

The cover hits the mark for a typical teen magazine—three smiling girls with bare shoulders and perfect teeth. The inside cover has an advertisement with a photo of an emaciated female teen promoting a book called *Diary of an Anorexic Girl*, also published by Transit Books.

Flip to page 198 and you will find an ad for an agency whose mission is to end homelessness. Go to page 33 and you can take one of many quizzes in the magazine/Bible. This one is entitled, "Do you have a healthy body image?" With multiple choice answers—"never, sometimes, often, always"—readers are asked to respond to the following ten statements:

1. I enjoy shopping for clothes.
2. I feel self-conscious when I am around someone I think is beautiful.
3. I love having my picture taken.
4. I try on a few different outfits before I finally decide what to wear.
5. I feel comfortable in a swimsuit.
6. When I look at myself in the mirror, I cringe.
7. There are parts of my body that I'm really proud of.
8. I am critical of other women's bodies, no matter how beautiful.
9. I eat what I want without really thinking about the fat or calories.
10. I weigh myself more than once a day.

At the bottom of the page you can rate yourself and tell if you have a "poor body image," "average body image," or "super body image."

Scattered throughout the 388-page New Testament are echoes of David Letterman's Top Ten Lists. On page 109 you can find a top ten list with the title "Random Ways to Make a Difference in Your Community." From number ten to number one they are: Do yard work for the elderly or sick. Donate your old clothes to needy families. Recycle cans and bottles. Use washable containers instead of plastic wrap for your lunch. Clip plastic rings on soda six packs. Offer to baby-sit your neighbors' kids for free. Drop a dollar in charity boxes. Smile freely. Pick up some else's litter. And the number one way to make a difference in your community is . . . Plant a tree.

Another top ten list is on page 294. The title is "Random Ways to Make a Difference in Your School." Again from number ten to number one they are: Pray for your school. Lead a Bible study. Take on a campus beautification project. Be nice to an underclassman. Have school spirit. Organize a group to raise money for charity. Help the cleaning staff after school hours. Pray for your teachers. Get involved; make some new friends. And the number one way to make a difference in your school is . . . Start a prayer club.

What I find remarkable is that telling someone the good news of how they can be forgiven of their sins and inherit eternal life with the true and living God did not make the top ten ways to make a difference either in the community or at school! According to the *Revolve* editors, planting a tree and beautifying a campus outrank the power and influence of the gospel of Jesus Christ.

On page 209, there is another interesting top ten list. The title is "Random Things to Look for in a Guy." From number ten to number one they are: Gentleness. Strength. Self-control. Loyalty. Friendship. Humor. Integrity. Leadership. Honesty. And the number one thing to look for in a godly guy is . . . Respect. Sadly, character traits like godliness, holiness, and spiritual maturity didn't make the top ten things a young woman should look for in a guy.

One more top ten list, please. On page 265 is a list with the heading, "Random Things to Know about Being a *Revolve* Girl." From number ten to number one they are: *Revolve* girls are fabulous friends. *Revolve* girls don't kiss and tell. *Revolve* girls enjoy spending time with family. *Revolve* girls are respectful of others. *Revolve* girls know their bodies are temples of God. *Revolve* girls should never gossip. *Revolve* girls are not argumentative. *Revolve* girls have good posture. *Revolve* girls don't talk with food in their mouths. And the number one way to be a *Revolve* girl is . . . *Revolve* girls don't call guys. (By the way, on this same page is a cartoon of Mary and Martha who are wearing low-riding jeans and skin-tight shirts and are sporting hourglass figures.)

Guys are a big deal in *Revolve*, so much so that there are call-out boxes all over the place with the picture of some hunk and his opinion. On page 9 there is a call-out box called "Guys Speak Out" with a question and an answer. The question is, "What should girls care about most when they're in high school?" The answer? "Probably school. It's the most important factor in helping you achieve your goals in life—more than looks or socializing." (So the authority is some guy? And what girls should care about most is *not* God?)

The shallowness continues with another call-out feature, found every few pages, called "Beauty Secrets." For example, on page 5 there is this tip: "As you apply your sunscreen, use that time to talk to God. Tell him how grateful you are for how he made you. Soon, you'll be so used to talking to him, it might become as regular and familiar as shrinking your pores."

One final example comes from the most famous verse in the Bible, John 3:16. On page 137, instead of including something about how to become a Christian, *Revolve* places this "Beauty Secret" alongside John 3:16: "When you pluck your eyebrows, it helps to start by placing a warm rag over them. This warms the pores so they are ready for the pain. Remember this if you ever have to break bad news to someone—a warm hug or kind words will help ease their pain. A good friend in times of need is a great comfort."

Agnieszka Tennant observes, "On page 186, the girls can find the 'Top Ten Great Christian Books.' C. S. Lewis and Dorothy Sayers haven't made the list. Top honors go to *Witnessing 101* by Tim Baker and published by Transit Books. In fact, all of the top ten books have been recently published by Thomas Nelson, most of them through Transit Books."[3]

Here's another curiosity: The eighth of the top ten great Christian books is titled *Why So Many Gods?* Its authors are Tim Baker and Kate Etue. Kate Etue is also the senior editor of *Revolve*. She was the one promoting the "biblezine" on CNN recently.[4]

What should we make of *Revolve*? It's not a magazine. It's not a Bible. It's certainly not a study Bible. Whaley says it is "an inspirational and motivational Bible product."[5]

Why should this pop-culture teen 'zine warrant our attention? Get this: It has broken all records for Thomas Nelson publishing for the most Bibles sold in the first month of publication—over 30,000! With this type of response, the company quickly printed another 70,000.

So, what are we to think about a New Testament packaged to resemble a fashion magazine?

First, I want to commend what I believe to be a good motive on the part of the designers. I support efforts to reach teenage girls with the life-transforming gospel contained in the New Testament. In fact, I have given almost twenty-five years of ministry to reaching teens with the gospel of Jesus Christ.

But let's ask some probing questions about propriety and wisdom. A Bible with dating tips, makeup secrets, top ten lists, and interviews with teenage boys—where did all this come from?

The creators unashamedly tell us. Laurie Whaley says,

> The research that we did with teens across the country indicated that they find the Bible to be very intimidating . . . and some of them even called it "freaky." . . . And so we asked them, "Well, what do you read?" And the response that came back was, "We read magazines." And so that was where the initial idea came to take the message of the Bible and to put it in a format in which teen girls were accustomed.[6]

In other words, the fundamental presupposition is that the gospel is best packaged in a culturally relevant way. But the Bible and its message are fundamentally countercultural. Russell Moore of The Southern Baptist Theological Seminary correctly points out, "The 'freakiness' of the Bible . . . is precisely what gives it the power to save. It is a message that is not glamorous at all. It is a message of a crucified and resurrected Christ who calls all people everywhere to reconciliation with God through Him. It is that otherness of the Bible that gives it its power."[7]

Os Guinness rightly observes,

By our uncritical pursuit of relevance we have actually courted irrelevance; by our breathless chase after relevance without a matching commitment to faithfulness, we have become not only unfaithful but irrelevant; by our determined efforts to redefine ourselves in ways that are more compelling to the modern world than are faithful to Christ, we have lost not only our identity but our authority and our relevance. Our crying need is to be faithful as well as relevant.[8]

The authority of the Bible is being eclipsed in practice by the assumptions of the modern world. By the way, the company has also released a magazine Bible aimed at teenage guys called *Refuel*. This guy-version of the Holy Book is a bit more explicit on sex and relationships. It also features articles on cars, music, the outdoors, sports, and money.

Is the church losing her identity and credibility? Are we trading the eternal for the temporal, the lasting for the trendy, the essential for the trivial, the transcendent for the transient, and the profound for the mundane?

Revolve is representative of contemporary attacks on the Bible that committed Christians must take seriously. Consider the following attacks on the Bible that *Revolve* unwittingly joins.

ADDING TO THE BIBLE

Let me be clear. The editors of *Revolve* have not added anything to the text of the New Testament—at least not explicitly. But putting all the call-out boxes with advice, even imperatives, within the context and covers of God's Word passes them off as authoritative.

These call-out additions are not the same as notes in a study Bible. Whereas a study Bible's notes are there to explain what the Scriptures say, these *Revolve* additions are there to add in what the Scriptures do not say. And the brains and wisdom from which this data comes is suspect.

Listen to these words from the *Revolve* web site:

Many teen girls are intimidated about reading the Bible.
However, *Revolve* makes the New Testament approachable and
helps readers understand biblical teaching through real life sce-
narios and familiar magazine features. To make the notes as relevant as possible, each has been written by women in their early
twenties who have spent time with young girls and know what
teens are looking for in life and from the Bible. Through this new
Bible format, young girls learn to approach family, friends and life
with Christian beliefs and morals, while at the same time not feeling excluded from pop culture.

In other words, the authorities are such because of their age (and
their ability to relate). Moreover, the advice they give is a self-help
therapy for fitting into pop culture. It is questionable whether or not
the target audience will have the discernment to distinguish between
the authority of the biblical text and that of the other "stuff." In effect,
then, non-biblical material is being added to the Bible.

EDITING THE BIBLE

At issue here is the translation, or rather the paraphrase, that is used.
The New Century Version is the text of choice for *Revolve*. It is not a
pure translation but rather a highly contemporized paraphrase that
overuses dynamic equivalence. As such, it is among the loosest in
relation to the original text.

God did not have a speech impediment when He spoke His
Word. He supernaturally froze the words, idioms, illustrations, and
allusions into His revelation. Resolving difficulties in understanding
the text is the job of the preacher, not the translators.

There is also a not-so-subtle commentary on the importance of
the Old Testament by its absence. The editors have commented that
it is too big and complicated for such a format. So, what are the criteria for printing God's Word—size and complication? If that is the
case, why did they choose to include the book of Revelation?

TRIVIALIZING THE BIBLE

At the heart of *Revolve* is the blatant attempt to package the words of Scripture to mirror the world as much as possible. But notice what is left out in the call-out boxes—how to die to yourself, how to treasure Jesus above all else, how to clearly explain the gospel to someone, and how to make your focus God rather than yourself!

Most of the "extra stuff" in *Revolve* is little more than can be found in *Vogue* or *Seventeen*. It is trivial and attempts to help girls with things that have nothing to do with the claims and challenges of the New Testament.

On the same page as John 20, where the resurrection is narrated, we find shopping tips! When the Gospel of Mark is introduced, it is called "the gospel for smarty pants." And on the same page where Paul discusses the incarnation of Jesus in Philippians 2, this "Beauty Secret" is found:

> Applying Foundation—You need a good, balanced foundation for the rest of your makeup, kinda like Jesus is the strong foundation in our lives. Keep him as the base, and build everything on him. If it doesn't fit in his plan for you, it will fall off the foundation. Everything else will fit where it needs to go.

This is no mere illustration—it is a trivializing of the precious reality of Christ being the foundation of all living for the Christian.

POLLUTING THE BIBLE

Flipping through *Revolve* is a bit like seeing a pure, pristine river with garbage floating down it. There is a contamination of the pure stream of God's truth and authority. Would Paul have thought it distasteful? Remember his words in 1 Corinthians 2:4-5: "my speech and my message were not in plausible words of wisdom, but in demonstration of the Spirit and of power, that your faith might not rest in the wisdom of men but in the power of God."

This biblezine puts man's wisdom (admittedly that of young men and women) parallel with the infinite value of Scripture. The stream of God's wisdom becomes polluted by things such as "Guys Speak Out."

In a "Guys Speak Out" section on page 128, the question is asked of a hunk-a-rific guy, "What's most important to you when looking for a girl?" The answer given does not center on God, Jesus, or even spiritual things. Rather, it is "a good personality, someone who takes care of herself." So what is the intended application for the average fifteen-year-old? Shockingly, it encourages young women to focus on themselves in order to please *guys*, rather than on *God!*

TEMPORALIZING THE BIBLE

Revolve attacks the eternality of the Word of God by making an edition that will be out-of-date in a very short time. Even the newspaper is out-of-date by tomorrow, and *Revolve* has so attached itself to the ever-changing culture that it is sure to have a short shelf-life. Ahhh, but therein is the financial genius. As soon as it is out-of-date, the publisher can update the pictures, tweak the advice—and whamo, another culturally relevant magazine.

There is a disturbing presupposition going unchecked here. Do we really have to be like the world to reach the world? Or do we really believe that the truth of God is eternal and that it has relevance for every culture, time, and place?

Scripture is transcendent. But *Revolve*'s emphasis on the here and now makes it inherently shallow.

REDIRECTING THE BIBLE

The Bible is about God. But the editors of *Revolve* have tried to redirect the attention to man. The first thing you see when you open the cover is an advertisement that is entirely man-centered.

Kate Etue, senior editor at Transit, says, "*Revolve* is the most innovative, revolutionary Bible product for this generation of teen girls. By mixing pop-culture fashion magazine formats with the eternal truth of Scripture, we've found a way to make the Word of God exciting, relevant and fun for young women again."[9]

Is the Bible's purpose to provide "fun for young women"? The editors seem to admit that the focus of *Revolve* is to make God's truth useful to girls. No well-meaning Christian would disagree with that motivation. But there is little mention of making much of God and the glory due His name.

NEUTRALIZING THE BIBLE

When Cindy Lauper sang her 1980s anthem "Girls Just Want to Have Fun," none of us in Evangelicalism thought that would end up being the criterion for the publication of Holy Scripture. The attempts to make the New Testament "fun" have taken the sting out of Scripture. Absent in the "extra stuff" is the profundity of truth, the weightiness of God, the otherworldliness of the Christian faith, and the awful reality of damning sin.

Listen to what Os Guinness says in this regard:

> The faith world of John Wesley, Jonathan Edwards, John Jay, William Wiberforce, Hannah More, Lord Shaftesbury, Catherine Booth, Hudson Taylor, D.L. Moody, Charles Spurgeon, Oswald Chambers, Andrew Murray, Carl Henry, and John Stott is disappearing. In its place a new evangelicalism is arriving in which therapeutic self-concern overshadows knowing God, spirituality displaces theology, end-times escapism crowds out day-to-day discipleship, marketing triumphs over mission, references to opinion polls outweigh reliance on biblical exposition, concerns for power and relevance are more obvious than concern for piety and faithfulness, talk of reinventing the church has replaced prayer for revival, and the characteristic evangelical passion for missionary enterprise is overpowered by the all-consuming drive to sustain the multiple business empires of the booming evangelical subculture.[10]

Do the editors at Transit Books really believe they have "found a way to make the Word of God exciting, relevant and fun"? And is this because of a fundamental belief that the Bible in its historical form is irrelevant? Modern Evangelicalism has now stooped to new lows with the release of *Revolve.* Yes, the Bible can be challenging to understand and apply. It takes hard work (2 Tim 2:15). But to mix God's truth with the kind of peripheral data in *Revolve* is to interfere with the paralyzing and penetrating shock of holy revelation on the sinful soul.

One final comment. It is terribly ironic that the very last call-out box in The *Revolve* New Testament is a brief commentary on Revelation 22:18. The box is entitled: "Learn It & Live It." It reads:

> Learn it: If anyone adds or takes away from the Scriptures, they will suffer disasters.
>
> Live it: Don't exaggerate when you talk about the Scriptures. *Don't mold them to fit your needs* [emphasis added].

May God shelter those behind The *Revolve* New Testament from such disasters.

PART THREE

Practicing Discernment in Your Local Church

ƧOLID ROCK? WHAT THE BIBLE ƧAYƧ ABOUT CONTEMPORARY WORƧHIP MUƧIC

John MacArthur

Sadly, Christians today need to exercise discernment in their local churches probably more than anywhere else. Whether due to poor preaching or a wrong philosophy of ministry, many local churches suffer because they lack the ability to distinguish sound doctrine from false teaching. To complicate matters, many believers have different opinions about preferential issues—sometimes causing unnecessary splits in the body of Christ. Discernment is needed for these situations as well, such that biblical principle and Christian grace may prevail. With this in mind, this chapter focuses on the often controversial topic of contemporary worship music. Should the church only sing hymns, should it only sing praise choruses, or should it land somewhere in the middle? And what are the biblical principles for determining these standards? This chapter addresses those very questions.

Recently I collaborated on a series of books about some of the greatest hymns of the Christian faith.[1] My task in the project was to write a doctrinal synopsis of each hymn we selected. It was a fascinating and enlightening exercise, causing me to delve more deeply than ever before into the rich heritage of Christian hymns.

As I researched the history of those hymns, I was reminded that a profound change took place in church music sometime near the end of the nineteenth century. The writing of hymns virtually stopped. Hymns were replaced by "gospel songs"—songs generally lighter in doctrinal content, with short stanzas followed by a refrain, a chorus, or a common final lyric line that was repeated after each stanza. Gospel songs as a rule were more evangelistic than hymns. The key difference was that most gospel songs were expressions of personal testimony aimed at an audience of people, whereas most of the classic hymns had been songs of praise addressed directly to God.

A NEW SONG

The style and form of the gospel song was borrowed directly from the popular music styles of the late nineteenth century. The man most commonly regarded as the father of the gospel song is Ira Sankey, a gifted singer and songwriter who rode to fame on D. L. Moody's coattails. Sankey was the soloist and music leader for Moody's evangelistic campaigns in America and Britain.

Sankey wanted a style of music that would be simpler, more popular, and better suited to evangelism than classic church hymns. So he began to write gospel songs—mostly short, simple ditties with refrains, in the style of the popular music of his day. Sankey would sing each verse as a solo, and the congregation would join each refrain. Although Sankey's music at first provoked some controversy, the form caught on worldwide almost immediately, and by the early part of the twentieth century precious few new hymns were being added to modern hymnbooks. Most of the new works were gospel songs in the genre Sankey had invented.

It is noteworthy that in most hymnbooks even today, the only well-known hymn with a copyright date after 1940 is "How Great Thou Art."[2] And to classify that work as a twentieth-century hymn is stretching things a bit. "How Great Thou Art" doesn't really follow the form of the classic hymns. It includes a refrain, which is more characteristic of gospel songs than of hymns. Moreover, it is not even really a twentieth-century work. The first three stanzas were originally written in 1886 by a well-known Swedish pastor, Carl Boberg, and translated from Swedish by British missionary Stuart Hine not long before the outbreak of World War II. Hine added the fourth stanza, which is the only verse in the popular English version of that hymn that was actually written in the twentieth century.[3]

In other words, for more than seventy years virtually no hymns have been added to the popular repertoire of congregational church music. That reflects the fact that very few true hymns of any enduring quality are being written.

My remarks are by no means meant as a blanket criticism of gospel songs. Many familiar gospel songs are wonderfully rich expressions of faith. Although Ira Sankey's most popular song, "The Ninety and Nine," is almost never sung as a congregational song today, it was the hit of Sankey's era. He improvised the music on the spot in one of Moody's mass meetings in Edinburgh, using the words from a poem he had clipped earlier that afternoon from a Glasgow newspaper. Those lyrics, written by Elizabeth Clephane, are a simple and moving adaptation of the Parable of the Lost Sheep from Luke 15:4-7.[4]

A more enduring favorite from the golden age of gospel songs is "Grace Greater than Our Sin."[5] The song is a celebration of the triumph of grace over our sin. Its refrain is familiar:

> *Grace, grace, God's grace,*
> *Grace that will pardon and cleanse within;*
> *Grace, grace, God's grace,*
> *Grace that is greater than all our sin!*

Songs like those have enriched the church's expressions of faith.

Frankly, however, many of the classic gospel songs are terribly weak in content in comparison to the hymns sung in earlier generations. In general, the rise of the gospel song in congregational singing signaled a diminishing emphasis on objective doctrinal truth and a magnification of subjective personal experience. The changing focus clearly affected the content of the songs. It is worth noting that some of the archetypical gospel songs are as vapid and vacuous as anything the hard-core opponents of the current generation of contemporary Christian music could ever legitimately complain about.

As a matter of fact, traditionalist critics who attack contemporary music merely because it is contemporary in style—especially those who imagine that the older music is always better—need to think through the issues again. And please understand that the concern I am raising has to do with content, not merely style.[6] Judging from lyrics alone, some of the most popular old-style music is even more offensive than the modern stuff. I can hardly think of a contemporary song that is more banal than the beloved old standby, "In the Garden":

I come to the garden alone,
While the dew is still on the roses;
And the voice I hear,
Falling on my ear,
The Son of God discloses.

And He walks with me, and He talks with me,
And He tells me I am His own;
And the joy we share as we tarry there
None other has ever known.

He speaks, and the sound of His voice
Is so sweet the birds hush their singing;
And the melody
That He gave to me
Within my heart is ringing.

I'd stay in the garden with Him
Tho the night around me be falling;

> *But He bids me go—*
> *Thru the voice of woe,*
> *His voice to me is calling.*[7]

Those lyrics say nothing of any real substance, and what they do say is not particularly Christian. It's a mawkish little rhyme about someone's personal experience and feelings—and even at that, it proclaims a pretty airy and ambiguous message. Whereas the classic hymns sought to glorify God, gospel songs such as "In the Garden" were glorifying raw sentimentality.

Numerous gospel songs suffer from the same kind of weaknesses. In fact, many of the very best-loved "old-fashioned" favorites are practically devoid of any truly Christian substance and are thick with sappy sentimentality. "Love Lifted Me," "Take My Hand, Precious Lord," "Whispering Hope," and "It Is No Secret What God Can Do" are some familiar examples that come quickly to mind.

Obviously, then, neither the antiquity nor the popularity of a gospel song is a good measure of its worthiness. And the fact that a gospel song is "old-fashioned" is quite clearly no guarantee that it is suited for edifying the church. When it comes to church music, older is not necessarily better.

In fact, these same "old-fashioned" gospel songs that are so often extolled by critics of modern church music are actually what paved the way for the very tendencies those critics sometimes rightly decry. In particular, the lack of substance in so much of today's music is the predictable fruit of the wholesale shift away from hymns to gospel songs, which began sometime in the late nineteenth century.

I'm not suggesting that the style of music Sankey introduced had no legitimate place. Gospel songs have no doubt played an important and effective evangelistic and testimonial role, and therefore they do deserve a prominent place in church music. But it was unfortunate for the church that by the start of the twentieth century, gospel songs were virtually all that was being written. Church musicians at the end of the nineteenth century (like the theologians of that era) were far too enamored with anything "modern." They embraced the new style of congregational music with unbridled aggressiveness, and in the process they all but discarded the old style of church hymns. Sadly, by the end of the century the gospel song had muscled in and elbowed out the classic hymn. And so the trend Sankey began all but ended the rich tradition of Christian hymnody that had flourished since the time of Martin Luther and even long before.

Prior to Sankey, the dominant hymn-writers had been pastors and theologians—men skilled in handling Scripture and sound doctrine.[8] With the shift to gospel songs, just about everyone with a flair for poetry felt he was qualified to write church music. After all, the new music was supposed to be personal testimony, not some kind of lofty doctrinal treatise.

Before Sankey's time, hymns were composed with a deliberate, self-conscious, didactic purpose. They were written to teach and reinforce biblical and doctrinal concepts in the context of worship directed to God. In other words, the kind of worship they embodied made demands on the human intellect. Those hymns aimed to praise God by extolling and proclaiming His truth in a way that enhanced the worshiper's comprehension of the truth. They set a standard of worship that was as cerebral as it was emotional. And that was perfectly biblical. After all, the first and great commandment teaches us to love God with all our heart, soul, and mind (Matt 22:37). It would never have occurred to our spiritual ancestors that worship was something to be done with a subdued intellect. The worship God seeks is worship in spirit and in truth (John 4:23-24).

But over the past century and a half, the popular concept of worship has changed as radically as the forms of music we sing. These days worship is often characterized as something that happens quite outside the realm of the intellect. This destructive notion has given rise to several dangerous movements in the contemporary church. It may have reached its pinnacle in the phenomenon known as the Toronto Blessing, where mindless laughter and other raw emotions were thought to constitute the purest form of worship and a visible proof of divine blessing.

As I have argued in several of my published works, I believe this modern notion of worship as a mindless exercise has taken a heavy toll in churches. It has led to a decreasing emphasis on preaching and teaching and an increasing emphasis on entertaining the congregation and making them feel good. All of this leaves the Christian in the pew untrained and unable to discern, and often blithely ignorant of the dangers all around.

Such anti-intellectualism has infected our music too. Or perhaps trite and frivolous music is what spawned so much anti-intellectualism in the first place. Indeed, it may be the case that modern church music has done more than anything else to pave the way for the sort of superficial, flippant, content-starved preaching that is rife today.

THE ERA OF THE PRAISE CHORUS

In the late twentieth century, another major shift occurred. Gospel songs gave way to a new form—the praise chorus. Praise choruses are pithy verses set to catchy music, generally shorter than gospel songs and with fewer stanzas.

Praise choruses, like hymns, are usually songs of praise addressed directly to God. So with this more recent shift came a return to pure worship (rather than testimony and evangelism) as the main focus and chief reason for congregational singing.

But unlike hymns, praise choruses generally have no didactic purpose. Praise choruses are meant to be sung as simple personal expressions of worship, whereas hymns are usually corporate expressions of worship with an emphasis on some doctrinal truth.[9] A hymn usually has several stanzas, each of which builds on or expands the theme introduced in the first stanza.[10] By contrast, a praise chorus is usually much shorter, with one or two verses, and most of these choruses make liberal use of repetition in order to prolong the focus on a single idea or expression of praise.

(Obviously, these are not absolute distinctions. Some praise choruses do contain doctrinal instruction, and some hymns are meant to be wonderfully personal expressions of simple praise.[11] But as a general rule, the classic hymns served a more deliberately didactic purpose than praise choruses do.)

There is certainly nothing wrong with the simple, straightforward personal praise that characterizes the best of today's praise choruses. Neither is there anything wrong with the evangelistic and testimonial thrust of yesterday's gospel songs. But it is a profound tragedy that in some circles, only contemporary choruses are sung. Other congregations limit their repertoire to hundred-year-old gospel songs. Meanwhile, a large and rich body of classic Christian hymnody is in danger of being utterly lost out of sheer neglect.[12]

*S*ONG*S*, HYMN*S*, AND *S*PIRITUAL *S*ONG*S*

The biblical prescription for Christian music is found in Colossians 3:16: "Let the word of Christ dwell in you richly, teaching and admonishing one another in all wisdom, singing psalms and hymns and spiritual songs, with thankfulness in your hearts to God."

That plainly calls for a variety of musical forms—"psalms and hymns and spiritual songs." Regarding the meaning of those expressions Charles Hodge wrote, "The early usage of the words psalmos, humnos, ode, appears to have been as loose as that of the corresponding English terms, psalm, hymn, song, is with us. A psalm was a hymn and a hymn a song. Still there was a distinction between them."[13]

A psalm spoke of a sacred song written for accompaniment with musical instrument. (*Psalmos* is derived from a word that denotes the plucking of strings with the fingers.) The word was used to designate the psalms of the Old Testament (cf. Acts 1:20; 13:33), as well as Christian songs (1 Cor 14:26).[14] A hymn spoke of a song of praise to God, a religious paean. A song, on the other hand, could be either sacred or secular music. So the apostle specifies "spiritual songs"— songs about spiritual things.

Precise distinctions between the terms are somewhat hazy, and as Hodge pointed out, that haziness is reflected even in our modern everyday usage of those words. But determining the actual forms of the early church's "psalms and hymns and spiritual songs" and making careful distinctions between the words is not essential, or Scripture would have recorded those distinctions for us.

The greater significance of the expression "psalms and hymns and spiritual songs" seems to be this: Paul was calling for a variety of musical forms and a breadth of spiritual expression that cannot be embodied in any one musical form. The strict psalms-only view (which is gaining popularity in some Reformed circles today) allows for none of that variety. The views of fundamentalist-traditionalists who seem to want to limit church music to the gospel-song forms of the early twentieth century would also squelch the variety Paul calls for. More significantly, the prevailing mood in modern evangelical churches—where people seem to want to binge on a steady diet of nothing but simplistic praise choruses—also destroys the principle of variety Paul sets forth here.

I believe the Protestant evangelical community erred a hundred years ago when the writing of hymns was almost completely abandoned in favor of gospel songs. The error was not the embracing of a new form. Again, the gospel-song form had a legitimate place in church music. But the error lay in utterly casting aside the rich heritage of hymns—along with the didactic, doctrinal richness of Christian music that had edified and sustained so many generations.

And I am convinced Christian songwriters today are making a similar mistake by failing to write substantial hymns while purging the old hymns from our congregational music repertoire and replacing them with trite praise choruses and pop-song look-alikes.

TEACHING AND ADMONISHING ONE ANOTHER

Too often forgotten by writers of praise choruses and other modern church music is the biblically mandated didactic role of church music. We're commanded to be "teaching and admonishing one another in . . . psalms and hymns and spiritual songs." Few modern praise choruses teach or admonish. Instead, most are written to stir the feelings only. They are too often sung like a mystical mantra—

with the deliberate purpose of putting the intellect into a passive state while the worshiper musters as much emotion as possible. Repetition is deliberately built into many praise songs precisely for this purpose.

The Vineyard paradigm of worship was virtually built on this principle. And churches worldwide have adopted the model. Consider this description of a typical modern worship service:

> Music . . . is limited exclusively to praise choruses—with lyrics shown on overhead projectors rather than sung out of books, so that the worshiper will have total freedom to respond physically. Each praise chorus is repeated several times, and the only signal that we're moving on to the next chorus is when the overhead changes. There is no announcement or spoken remarks between songs—indeed, no song leader, so the singing has a spontaneous feel to it.
>
> The music starts slow and soft and builds gradually but steadily in a 45-minute crescendo. Each successive chorus has a more powerful emotional tone than the previous one. Over the course of 45 minutes, the emotional power of the music increases by almost imperceptible degrees from soft and gentle to a powerful, driving intensity. At the beginning everyone is seated. As the feeling of fervor increases, people respond almost as if on cue, first by raising hands, then by standing, then by kneeling or falling prostrate on the floor. At the end of the worship time fully half the congregation are on the carpet, many lying face-down and writhing with emotion. The music has been carefully and purposefully brought to this intense emotional peak. One senses that this is the whole purpose of the congregational singing—to elevate emotions to a white-hot fervor. The more intense the feeling, the more people are convinced they have truly "worshiped."

Yet in all this there is no particular emphasis on the content of the songs. We sing about "feeling" God's presence among us, as if our rising emotions are the chief way His presence is confirmed and the force of His visitation is measured. Several of the songs tell the Lord He is great and worthy of praise, but none ever really says why. No matter; the goal clearly is to stir our emotions, not to focus our minds on any particular aspect of God's greatness. In fact, later in the sermon, the preacher cautions us against following our heads rather than our hearts in any of our dealings with God.

In other words, the worship here is intentionally and purposefully anti-intellectual. And the music reflects it. While there is nothing overtly erroneous about any of the praise choruses that were sung, there is nothing of substance in most of them either. They are written to be vehicles of passion, because passion—deliberately divorced from the intellect—is what defines this concept of "worship."[15]

Not all contemporary church worship goes that far, of course, but the most popular trends are decidedly in that direction. Anything too cerebral is automatically suspect, deemed not "worshipful" enough, because the prevailing notion of worship frankly gives little or no place to the intellect. That's why in the typical church service sermons are being shortened and lightened and more time is being given to music. Preaching, which used to be the centerpiece of the worship service, is now viewed as something distinct from worship, something that actually intrudes on the "praise and worship time," in which the focus is music, testimony, and prayer—but mostly music, and music whose main purpose is to stir the emotions.

But if music's proper function includes "teaching and admonishing," then music in the church ought to be much more than an emotional stimulant. In fact, this means music and preaching should have the same aim. Both properly pertain to the proclamation of God's Word. Preaching is properly seen as an aspect of our worship. And conversely, music is properly seen as an aspect of the ministry of the Word, just like preaching. Therefore the songwriter ought to be as skilled in Scripture and as concerned for theological precision as the preacher. Even more so, because the songs he writes are likely to be sung again and again (unlike a sermon that is preached only once).

I fear that perspective is utterly lost on the average church musician these days. As Leonard Payton has observed,

> So extreme is the case now that anyone who knows half a dozen chords on a guitar and can produce rhymes to Hallmark card specifications is considered qualified to exercise this component of the ministry of the Word regardless of theological training and examination.[16]

Payton points out that the leading Old Testament musicians (Heman, Asaph, and Ethan, 1 Chron 15:19) were first of all Levitical priests, men who had devoted their lives to the Lord's service (cf. v. 17), men trained in the Scriptures and skilled in handling the Word of God. Their names are listed as authors of some of the inspired psalms (cf. Pss 73—83; 88; 89). Payton writes,

> It was Asaph who thundered that God owns "the cattle on a thousand hills" (Ps. 50:10). If the modern church musician wrote a worship text like Psalm 50, he would probably not get it published in the contemporary Christian music industry, and he might be on the fast track to getting fired at his church. Heman's Psalm 88 is incontestably the bleakest of all the Psalms. All this to say, Levitical musicians wrote Psalms, and those Psalms were not obligated to the gnostic, emotional demands of twentieth-century evangelical church music.[17]

First Kings 4:31 says of Solomon, "He was wiser than all other men, wiser than Ethan the Ezrahite, and Heman." Payton observes the significance of that statement:

> If Solomon hadn't been in the land, two musicians would have been the wisest men. In short, musicians were teachers of the highest order. This leads me to suspect that Levitical musicians, being scattered through the land, served as Israel's teachers. Furthermore, the Psalms were their textbook. And because this textbook was a songbook, it may well be that the Levitical musi-

cians catechized the nation of Israel through the singing of psalms.[18]

Like it or not, today's songwriters are teachers too. Many of the lyrics they are writing will soon be far more deeply and permanently ingrained in the minds of Christians than anything they hear their pastors teach from the pulpit. How many songwriters are skilled enough in theology and Scripture to qualify for such a vital role in the catechesis of our people?

The question is answered by the paucity of expression found in many of today's praise choruses—especially when compared to some of the classic hymns. Although not true in every case, the theological depth that generally characterizes contemporary praise choruses is not as profound and not as precise. In fact, for some songs it might be appropriate to ask if the contemporary church is collectively guilty of dishonoring God with our faint praise.

By contrast, read the final stanza of a classic hymn of worship, "Immortal, Invisible." After reviewing a fairly comprehensive list of the divine attributes, the lyricist wrote:

> *Great Father of glory, pure Father of light,*
> *Thine angels adore Thee, all veiling their sight;*
> *All praise we would render—O help us to see*
> *'Tis only the splendor of light hideth Thee!*[19]

Both the poetry and the sense are superior to almost everything being written today.

Again, my major concerns have to do more with the content than with the style of church music. But style and artistry are important too. Why aren't we more scandalized when someone performs bad music in church than we are when someone hangs bad art in a gallery? Offering tawdry songs to God is certainly a greater travesty than displaying a lousy painting in an art gallery. There is no place for mediocrity in our worship of the Most High God. That means not everyone who wants to write or perform music in the church ought to be given a platform. Some people's art simply doesn't deserve to be exhibited.

Modern songwriters clearly need to take their task more seriously. Churches should also do everything they can to cultivate excellent musicians who are thoroughly trained in handling the Scriptures and able to discern sound doctrine. Most important, pastors and elders need to begin exercising closer and more careful oversight of the church music ministry, consciously setting a high standard for the doctrinal and biblical content of what we sing. If those things are done, I believe we'll begin to see a dramatic qualitative difference in the music that is being written for the church.

In the meantime, let's not throw out the classic hymns. Better yet, let's revive some of the ones that have fallen into disuse and add them once again to our repertoire.

In bringing this chapter to a close, I would like to include a short article written by Nathan Busenitz entitled "A Checklist for Church Music." Nathan provides a list of ten helpful questions that Christians can ask as they seek to discern the good from the bad in contemporary worship music.

ADDENDUM: A CHECKLIST FOR CHURCH MUSIC

What type of music is appropriate for church worship services? While the question is simple enough, the answers given are often both complex and controversial. Yet, the question is a crucial one to consider because music is a central part of Christian worship. If our music does not please the Lord, neither will the worship that music is intended to produce.

So how can churches be God-honoring in the music they use? In order to answer this question correctly, we must begin by looking to the principles of God's Word. Neither personal preferences nor cultural trends can be our guide. Even in the area of music, Scripture must be our authority.

Below are ten questions that pastors and church leaders (along with the congregation as a whole) should ask about the worship music they use. Drawn directly from biblical principles, these questions may not answer every specific case, but they do provide a theological checklist for examining church music.

1. Is your church music God-focused? Without question, true worship must be God-centered (Exod 20:3-6), for He alone is worthy of our praise (Ps 148:13). He deserves our most fervent devotion and our highest priority. He is our exalted King, and He must have center stage. Anything short of God-centered worship is idolatry (cf. Jer 2:13, 27-28), and false worship is clearly unacceptable (Deut 12:29-31; 16:21-22; Gal 5:19-21).

Because the purpose of church music is to provide a vehicle for worship, it must be God-focused rather than man-centered (cf. Ps 27:6; 150:3-4). Any other purposes or priorities are secondary. From the style and performance to the audience and their reaction, nothing should ever usurp God's place as the supreme object of our affection. Because biblical worship demands a God-centered focus, church music (if it is to legitimately be called worship music) must begin and end with Him.

2. Does your church music promote a high view of God? It is not enough for church music to merely focus on God, if the view of God presented is inadequate. Too many Christian songs come dangerously close to violating the commandment, "You shall not take the name of the LORD your God in vain" (Exod 20:7) by treating Him in a common, almost mundane fashion.

Music that is worthy of our Savior must promote an accurate and exalted view of who He is (cf. Isa 40:12-26). Throughout Scripture, all who encountered the living God were radically changed (Moses in Exod 33—34; Isaiah in Isa 6; Peter, James, and John during the Transfiguration in Matt 17). There was nothing ordinary about the Lord they saw or the trembling worship-filled response they had. Our music then, if it is to facilitate heartfelt worship, must clearly convey the majesty, glory, and honor of God (cf. Heb 10:31; Rom 11:33-36; Rev 14:7).

3. Is your church music orderly? The God whom we serve is a God of order. This is most clearly seen in His creation of the world, where He brought form and function out of a watery mass (Gen 1; cf. Rom 1:20). It is no surprise, then, that the apostle Paul commands the Corinthians that "all things [in the church] should be done decently and in order" (1 Cor 14:40).

Along these same lines, Ephesians 5:18 commands believers to continually be under the control of the Holy Spirit at all times. Church music, then, should never encourage participants to exchange the control of the Spirit for the control of some other force—be it emotional, psychological, or other. Rather, church members are to be under the influence of the Spirit-empowered Word of God (cf. Col 3:16). Mindless emotionalism, often hyped up by repetition and "letting go," comes closer to the paganism of the Gentiles (cf. Matt 6:7) than to any form of biblical worship.

4. Is the content of your church music biblically sound? While instrumental music is certainly appropriate during the worship service (cf. 2 Chron 5:13), most church music includes lyrical content. At the very least, these lyrics should be both intelligible and biblically accurate—readily conveying scriptural truth to all who sing them (cf. Eph 5:19-20).

Beyond being accurate, lyrics should also be clear and in keeping with the biblical context. For example, songs that come from the Old Testament (even when the lyrics are directly cited from a passage) should not be made to apply to the church today if they only apply to Israel before Christ. (An excellent example of this is when Psalm 51:11 is sung without any explanation of the context.)

Lyrics should never be trite or flippant in their treatment of great biblical themes. Instead, church music (no matter the style) should deepen the biblical and theological understanding of the congregation. A song that is inaccurate, out-of-context, or trite only hinders the spiritual growth of those who sing it.

5. Does your church music promote unity in your church? As noted above, the primary goal of church music is worship. Yet, Scripture also speaks of Christian songs as a form of edification (1 Cor 14:26; Eph 5:19-20). Because the church is a body

(1 Cor 12), our worship toward God includes our service toward others (Rom 12:1-9).

The goal of corporate worship then is to glorify God while serving others. With this in mind, the right approach to church music never selfishly demands personal preference, but always looks out for the interests of others (Phil 2:1-4). Moreover, if something we do tempts a fellow Christian to fall into sin, we must proceed with great caution and care (Rom 14; 1 Cor 8).

6. Is your church music performed with excellence? Church music, along with everything else we do, should be done for the glory and honor of God (1 Cor 10:31). As our perfect Master and loving Father, He certainly deserves the very best that we can offer. To give Him anything less falls far short of what He demands. Even Old Testament Israel was expected to give the first and the best to the Lord (cf. Lev 1—7; Num 18:32).

Needless to say, if it bears His name, it's worth our best. While a church may not have the resources to hire a full orchestra or recruit a large band, the music should still be done wholeheartedly and with excellence. Music that is not sincere, from a pure heart, is not worship (Ps 24:3-4; Amos 5:23). And music that is done without excellence is usually distracting, thereby taking away from the God-centered atmosphere essential to true worship.

7. Does your church music prepare your people for the preaching of God's Word? Second Timothy 4:2 commands us to "preach the Word." Just a few verses earlier, the apostle Paul expounds on the sufficiency of Scripture and its importance in our lives (2 Tim 3:16-17). It is only through God's Word that we learn about Him; it is only through the Bible that God reveals Himself to us. The Scripture, therefore, must be the centerpiece of corporate worship—providing both the construct and the climax.

For this reason, times of singing (when God's people speak to Him) should never overshadow or eclipse preaching (when God speaks to His people through His Word). Instead, worship through song should complement the proclamation of the truth. Church music that takes place before the sermon should prepare the congregation for what the Holy Spirit wants them to hear. And church music that follows the sermon should be an appropriate response to what has just been received (cf. Col 3:16-17).

8. Does your church music adorn the gospel of Jesus Christ? The New Testament model of church life implies that the local assembly is to primarily function as a place of worship and edification (cf. Acts 2:41-42). Evangelism, on the other hand, is expected of believers as they go throughout the rest of their daily activities (Matt 28:18-20).

This being said, the local church (as an assembly of Christians) must still present a good testimony before a watching world (cf. 1 Cor 14:23-25). After all, Paul commands us to "adorn the doctrine of God our Savior . . . in everything" (Titus 2:10), and Peter exhorts us to "proclaim the excellencies" of God (1 Pet 2:9). Church music, then, should be a wonderful witness to the greatness of our Lord and Savior. It should never tarnish His reputation or confuse unbelievers as to what the gospel teaches.

9. Does your church music promote passionate worship? As noted earlier, church music must be God-focused, reverently presenting Him in all of His majesty. At the same time, it should never be boring, dry, or stale. After all, God is not boring. And heaven (where the primary occupation is worship) is also not boring (cf. Rev 4—5).

While maintaining a proper respect for God, biblical worship is always brimming with personal passion and Christ-exalting emotion (cf. 1 Chron 15:29; 16:4-6). Of course, the expression of this passion will manifest itself differently in different congregations. Furthermore, this passion must be expressed in an orderly, Spirit-controlled manner. Nonetheless, passionless worship—sounding more like a lullaby than a glorious anthem—is not really worship at all (John 4:23).

10. Is your church's philosophy of music based on biblical principles? Although numerous preferences and opinions exist, your church's philosophy of music must be based on biblical principles. Church leaders should not simply adhere to certain standards because they have always done so. Nor should they blindly permit just any type of music to be played in their church services. Instead, they should search the Scriptures (like the Bereans of Acts 17:11), determining the biblical principles that undergird a right philosophy of music in worship.

Once the principles have been established, the music leader has the liberty to apply those principles in different ways depending on the specific needs of his congregation. In the end, pastors must be careful not to exalt personal preference to the same level as biblical principle, or to ignore biblical principles under the assumption that everything about church music is preferential.

JUST AS I AM: A CLOSER LOOK AT INVITATIONS AND ALTAR CALLS

Carey Hardy

Public invitations and altar calls are a regular part of many church services. Usually included at the end of the service, they provide the congregation with an opportunity to respond to the message. Often this response is associated with a conversion experience. But altar calls can also be used for other reasons: to rededicate one's life to the Lord, to commit oneself to specific Christian service, or to join a local church. This chapter, adapted from a Shepherds' Conference seminar, investigates this practice from a biblical perspective. By applying discernment to church programs and philosophies such as this, believers will be better able to minister with the confidence that they are pleasing God.

It is a familiar scene in many American churches. As the sermon ends, music begins playing softly in the background. The preacher prays and then begins talking softly to his congregation. "With every head bowed and every eye closed," he says as he invites those who are feeling convicted by the sermon to quietly slip up their hands. "No one is looking around," he reminds his audience.

After a few moments he continues, "If you've raised your hand, look up here to me so I can talk directly to you. I don't want to embarrass you; I just want to talk to you." Those who have lifted up their hands are then asked to leave their seats and make their way down the aisle where a designated counselor can meet with them.

At any point in this approach, an invitation hymn is sung—whether it's "Just As I Am," "I Surrender All," "Have Thine Own Way," or another well-known gospel song. After singing through several verses of the hymn, the minister may ask for the instruments to continue playing quietly. This gives those who have come forward the opportunity to pair off with a counselor, while also providing those in the audience, who are still resisting, one more opportunity to respond "before it's too late." When it becomes clear that no one else is coming forward, the service ends with one final verse of the chosen hymn.

WHAT ARE ALTAR CALL*S*?

Commonly known as the "altar call," this practice does not always follow the exact pattern described above. But in general it is the time at the close of the sermon when, usually during some form of music, listeners are invited to come to the front in response to the message. As such, altar calls can serve a variety of purposes. Joining the church, repenting from sin, and coming to faith in Christ might each be facilitated by an altar call, depending on the church and the occasion.

Although its exact starting point is debated, most agree that the practice came into prominence in the 1830s under the leadership and influence of Charles Finney. He popularized this approach through what he called "the mourner's bench" or "anxious seat." Others in history, such as Billy Sunday, D. L. Moody, and Billy Graham, followed Finney's example and contributed to its widespread acceptance. In fact, in terms of the altar call we see today, Billy Graham's method has been most influential.

WHAT REASONS ARE GIVEN TO SUPPORT ALTAR CALLS?

At least four basic arguments are used to support altar calls and public invitations. First, many contend that we should use this method because Christ used it. In other words, Christ called people publicly, so we should do the same. This argument is bolstered by texts such as Matthew 10:32 ("So everyone who acknowledges me before men, I also will acknowledge before my Father who is in heaven") and the "Follow me" passages of the Gospels (cf. Matt 19:21; Mark 1:17; 2:14).

A second argument suggests that a formal, public response reinforces the decisions people make. When they walk down to the front, it settles their commitment and seals it in their heart. Because they took the step publicly, in front of an affirming congregation, it is more likely to be real and irrevocable.

A third argument is that altar calls are necessary because they provide an easy, organized way to present new converts to the congregation while also inviting non-members to join. In other words, unless there is an altar call at the end of the service, there is no way for people to publicly profess Christ and join with the local body.

Fourth, and finally, many believe that altar calls provide the church with a visual demonstration (or proof) that God is working. Whether saved or unsaved, those in the congregation are able to see God at work. When men, women, and children flock down the aisles at the end of a service, believers in the audience are encouraged to witness God's power on display. At the same time, unbelievers are convicted by the testimony of those who have responded.

WHAT CAUTIONS SHOULD CHRISTIANS CONSIDER REGARDING ALTAR CALLS?

At first glance, the four reasons listed above are quite convincing. Christ did invite people publicly. Some people could appear to be helped, in their own resolve, by being invited publicly. Perhaps the church is benefited, practically speaking, when people are invited publicly. And both believers and unbelievers could be spiritually impacted when those around them respond to a public invitation.

But are altar calls really the best method of evoking change in people's hearts? For that matter, are they even a biblical method? In answer to these questions, and in response to the supporting arguments given above, at least seven concerns need to be considered.

1. *The modern invitation system lacks true biblical support.* We must begin by noting that there are no clear biblical precedents or commands for altar calls. It's true that Jesus did make statements such as "Follow me" and "If you confess me before men, I will confess you before my Father, who is in heaven." But it is certainly a stretch to conclude from these passages that Jesus gave altar calls. Jesus clearly called people to follow Him (and we should also call people to follow Christ), but this is not the same as asking someone to "come forward" or "walk the aisle" as a testimony of the decision they have made. Truth be told, Jesus never spoke in terms of a one-time decision that you make about Him but rather exhorted His hearers to follow Him wholeheartedly for all of their lives. Christ was calling people to a life that continually confesses Him before men. We do not find in Scripture that the test of discipleship is a one-time decision.

A. W. Tozer is an example of a great preacher who understood this. Listen to the following account, recorded by Earl Swanson, about a sermon Tozer delivered in Long Beach, California:

> As he came to the conclusion of his message the air was totally electrified. I was accustomed to altar calls and was fully expecting to see a mass movement forward. That surely would have been the case, had he chosen to do so. Rather, he announced: "Don't come down here to the altar and cry about it; you go home and live it."[1]

That certainly reflects Jesus' attitude in the Gospels. He was far more concerned about people living out their Christian commitment than He was about having them come forward. To be sure, Christ did challenge large crowds of people to follow Him. But to say that Jesus used altar calls (or to use His call as the basis for altar calls) is frankly a dishonest use of Scripture.

2. *"Coming to faith" is often confused with "coming down the aisle."* A second concern with altar calls is this: The act of coming forward and the moment of salvation can be wrongly confused. Even those who use altar calls admit this problem—people can leave trusting the wrong thing. Of course, genuine attempts are often made to clarify that "going down the aisle" doesn't save anybody. Unfortunately, in many cases the confusion still lingers.

For example, it's not uncommon for a pastor or evangelist to plead with folks to come to the front "to give your life to Christ." In another setting they might be telling people something else, that coming forward is merely a testimony of the experience that an individual has already had with Christ.

So when is the person converted? Is it when they come forward, before they come forward, or when they pray with the counselor they meet at the altar? Is it coming forward to receive salvation, or is it a testimony of a conversion that's already taken place?

Because altar calls leave the actual point of conversion unclear, the practice can confuse and misguide Christians. Biblical distinctives—such as repentance, belief, and trust—potentially end up being overlooked or replaced, because the emphasis is on "coming forward" rather than on turning from sin to Christ. Even the popular sinner's prayer (where people are instructed to "let Jesus come into your heart") is a poor substitute for the biblical gospel. Christ's message to sinners was, "Repent and believe!" He did not allow other man-made techniques or methodologies to cloud the clear intent of His message. Altar calls often put too much weight on the act of "walking an aisle," while the biblical essentials for true conversion are minimized or completely ignored.

3. *Altar calls risk giving false assurance to the unconverted.* When altar calls are used, especially in respect to evangelism, it is typical to give immediate assurance to those who come forward. As long as they've made some sort of decision, they are quickly paraded before the congregation as "part of God's family." As a result, the public invitation

leads people to believe that what brings them into a right standing with God is their *decision*. Altar calls are clearly decision-oriented. And once individuals have made their decision, they are told to never doubt it.

Sometimes this decision-oriented assurance is taken to extremes. One well-known teacher, for example, talks about going to the back-yard and driving a stake into the ground. The logic here is that any-time you doubt your salvation, you should simply look at that stake and remember that you settled it with God. But how can a stick in the dirt settle anything? This type of thinking is dangerous because it deceives people into resting their faith on a profession rather than resting it on Christ, who alone is able to save forever (see Heb 7:25).

Scripture makes a very sober statement about those who think they're saved when they're not. Matthew 7:23 states that the Lord will say to many, "I never knew you." The reason the invitation system is so dangerous lies in the fact that it leads people to base their eternal salvation on a one-time confession. And this decision is accepted as evidence of salvation, even when the individual continues to live a life of sin and rebellion. In other words, his or her assurance is coming from an act on his or her part rather than from a *trust* in the promises of God, the sacrifice of Christ, and the sanctifying work of the Holy Spirit. Such persons can point to a date when they walked down the aisle, but if someone pressed them hard enough, it would be very dif-ficult for them to point out some proof of regeneration now.

Biblically speaking, the Holy Spirit, using Scripture, is the One who gives assurance. It's not the evangelist or any other person who gives assurance. As human beings, we can't save anybody, we can't keep them saved, and we can't, ultimately, assure them that they are saved. We can, however, show them what the Bible says about assur-ance and then trust the Holy Spirit.

George Whitefield had it right when he said:

There are so many stony ground hearers, who receive the Word with joy, that I have determined to suspend my judgment till I know the tree by its fruits. I cannot believe they are converts until I see fruit brought back; it will never do a sincere soul any harm.[2]

Along these same lines, Charles Spurgeon warned:

> Sometimes we are inclined to think that a very great portion of modern revivalism has been more a curse than a blessing, because it has led thousands to a kind of peace before they have known their misery; restoring the prodigal to the Father's house and never making him say, "Father, I have sinned." It very often happens that the converts that are born in excitement die when the excitement is over.[3]

So what does this mean for pastors and evangelists today? Does it mean that we should stop proclaiming the gospel? Of course not. But it does mean that we must be careful not to give assurance to those who show no evidence of conversion. Just because someone walks down an aisle and prays a prayer doesn't necessarily mean that they have been genuinely saved.

4. *Many who are "converted" during altar calls fall away.* Sparing people from false assurance becomes even more important when one considers the high number of altar-call "converts" who never produce any spiritual fruit in their lives. They claim to be Christians because they walked an aisle, but their long-term behavior suggests just the opposite.

Leighton Ford argues that "the inner decision for Christ is like driving a nail through a board. The open declaration of that [going forward] is like clinching the nail on the other side, so that it can not be easily pulled out."[4] If this were actually true, it would seem that the invitation system would be producing a *higher* percentage of converts faithfully living for the Lord. It ought to be helping the problem—resulting in a life of spiritual fruit.

Sadly, in contrast to Ford's optimism, those who look honestly at statistics related to crusade altar calls know that a minority of those who have made decisions display any signs of conversion even a few weeks after their altar call experience. With this in mind, R. L. Dabney once commented that most people in his day had come "to coolly accept the fact that forty-five out of fifty, or even a higher ratio, will eventually apostatize."[5]

This is not to say that no one can be saved during an altar call. But when this happens, it's not because of the altar call or the sinner's prayer. Instead, it is the work of God quickening the heart, in spite of whether or not there is an altar call.

The point remains: Those who use altar calls will have both kinds of conversions—the true and the false. The problem is that both are presented to the church as being genuine. And this type of confusion can have serious consequences, especially for those who are basing their assurance in a false profession.

5. *Altar calls are often based more on emotional manipulation than biblical conviction.* Altar calls are, no doubt, effective at bringing crowds to the front of the stage. In fact, the techniques that altar calls use are effective, even when no biblical truth is being presented. It could be a political meeting or a fund-raiser for a local charity group. Either way, the altar call method can be tacked on to energize the crowd and encourage them to commit. If the music is soft enough, the lighting is just right, and the speaker is passionate and persuasive, the altar call can be used to promote any message or cause. But can we call a method like this biblical when the content of the gospel is not essential to the method?

Along these lines, I am personally reminded of the worst altar call I've ever witnessed. This is certainly an extreme example, but I think it makes the point. I was helping with a vacation Bible school once where, as is typical, each day of the week, for half a day, we would teach the kids the Bible. And every day, toward the end of our time, we would take the older kids to the auditorium and hold a special service where the gospel would be clearly and passionately presented.

At the end of the week, the last message included an extended altar call, giving these kids an invitation to respond to the gospel they had heard all week. But the extreme nature of this particular altar call took me by surprise.

A staff pastor set two galvanized trash cans on the stage. One can was marked "Heaven," and one was marked "Hell." Each child was given a card and was told to write his or her name on it. The pastor then gave the instructions, "I want you to form a line. Then come by and drop your card, either in the can marked 'Heaven' or the one marked 'Hell.' Make your decision now. Make your choice."

To make things worse, in the one marked "Hell" he literally built a fire. There in the worship center, of all places, flames and smoke were spewing out of this galvanized trash can! Needless to say, the kids' response was overwhelming. All of those children got saved! Or did they? In many cases, probably not. They were merely responding (as any human being would) to the manipulative techniques of the altar call.

When I witnessed that altar call, I was deeply grieved. The power of the gospel was usurped by a scare tactic. The results may have included a high number of decisions, but I doubt there were very many true conversions. The message could have been anything, and the results would have been similar.

6. *Scripture already explains how to make a profession of faith public.* Many pastors are quick to publicly introduce the one who has prayed as a new brother or sister in Christ. Sometimes this introduction comes within minutes of the last verse of the invitation hymn. The pastor or evangelist may not have even known the individual until that moment. Yet the church is told to wholeheartedly embrace him or her as part of the family, no questions asked.

But is this the only method for introducing new converts publicly? Or does God's Word prescribe a better method? I believe the answer to that second question is "yes," and it comes in two parts.

First, there is believer's baptism—an ordinance given to us by Jesus Christ. Many churches, at the baptismal service, give converts the opportunity to verbally testify to God's work in their life. At this time they are publicly identified with the body of Christ. Walking an aisle is not God's prescribed method of public identification with Christ; baptism is.

Second, new believers make their confession public by living their lives for the glory of God. The changing power of Christ is a powerful public testimony. And churches don't need altar calls to add members to the congregation. There are various ways to do this. Some churches, for example, have developed a process of membership—complete with interviews (where aspiring members give their testimony), classes (about the church and the importance of serving), and a final public presentation to the congregation at a worship service. The point is that churches that do not use altar calls have no trouble presenting new members to the church.

7. *Altar calls suggest a lack of trust in God's sovereignty.* A final concern with public invitations is that they often indicate a lack of trust in divine sovereignty—specifically in the area of evangelism. This lack of confidence is sometimes heard in comments such as "If we don't provide an opportunity for people to respond to the gospel, someone might leave and never have another opportunity to be saved. Then their blood will be on our hands. They could die in an accident this week, and their eternal judgment in Hell is our fault." What a burden to live under, thinking that somebody's eternal destiny is in our hands. Did we say the right words, preach the right sermon, and give enough time for the altar call? This is not a pressure that we were meant to bear.

But this type of guilt is never supposed to be our motivation for evangelism. Sometimes sermons and revivals use manipulation like this to urge people to evangelize. And the people are emotionally moved because they feel guilty for not witnessing to their neighbors. Of course, there's always a story told about somebody somewhere who failed to witness, and then a friend died in a car accident the next day. As a result, people begin to put pressure on themselves and on others.

But where is God's sovereignty in all of this? Scripture makes it clear that salvation is of the Lord—every aspect of it—and that those whom the Lord has foreknown and predestined, He does indeed call and justify, and whom He justifies, He will indeed someday glorify. Salvation is presented in Scripture as *completed* from God's perspective. Our role is faithfulness and obedience to the Lord. If we're not faithful to evangelize and to call people to repentance, that is sin on our part. But the eternal destiny of a soul is in God's hands, not ours. It is His job to convert sinners. Ours is simply to be faithful.

In chapter 14 of his classic book *Preaching and Preachers,* Martyn Lloyd-Jones commented on altar calls, saying, "this method surely carries in it the implication that sinners have an inherent power of decision and of self-conversion."[6] Lloyd-Jones is pointing out that, in addition to diminishing the sovereignty of God, those who utilize altar calls have an inadequate understanding of biblical anthropology. It is a false assumption to think that man has the ability, on his own, to make a decision to trust in Christ for his salvation. Man is completely tainted by the Fall! Some people in church history, though, such as Thomas Aquinas, taught that everything about man was affected by the Fall except his reasoning ability. Thus, intellectual arguments for God's existence were crafted with the presupposition that if you present the evidence clearly enough, you can convince sinners to convert. But such thinking denies a biblical view of man, giving far too much credit to fallen human beings. Their will is in bondage, and their minds are darkened. All are born totally depraved; they are blind unless the Holy Spirit opens their eyes (cf. 1 Cor 2:14). God therefore has to do a supernatural work in an individual for him to believe the gospel.

Lloyd-Jones continued:

> There is an implication here that the evangelist somehow is in a position to manipulate the Holy Spirit and His work. [So] often today organizers are able to predict the number of "results." [However] this method tends to produce a superficial conviction of sin, if any at all. People often respond because they have the impression that by doing so they will receive certain benefits.[7]

Certainly, the doctrine of regeneration is brought into question. "This," Lloyd-Jones writes, "is the most serious thing of all. [Regeneration] is the work of the Holy Spirit, and His work alone, no one else can do it. And as it is His work, it is always a thorough work; and it is always a work that will show itself."[8] That's the bottom line. John MacArthur, talking about Paul's comments in 1 Corinthians 2, echoes the position of Lloyd-Jones.

[Paul] didn't use techniques that excite and stir, and move people's emotions to achieve results. He preached the Scriptures to the mind. Many preachers today know how to move people to respond without the Scriptures being the issue. They can manipulate them emotionally, and frankly, that kind of stuff really prostitutes the preacher's stewardship, because it makes him no different then a secular persuader.

Preachers who are gifted communicators, and who are articulate, and use the emotional techniques, and the sad stories, and the tear-jerking approaches, and who get the mood music playing behind the scene—[they] can create the kind of manipulative environment, and can effect in people behavior changes and even alter their basic values, and never need to use the Word of God. But what is the ultimate result? Is it true regeneration? Of course not! The only legitimate tool is the Scripture. The only legitimate bridge to change is the mind.

I'm not saying that people can't be converted during an altar call. But I am saying that people who aren't being converted get swept up in it. The people who are converted, are converted because they comprehend the truth and because the Spirit of God effects the transformation.[9]

DOES THIS MEAN WE STOP EVANGELIZING?

From a biblical and theological standpoint, altar calls are fraught with areas of concern. They have no scriptural basis. They confuse the essence of the gospel. They often produce false professors. They offer false assurance to many. They rely on manipulative techniques. They don't follow the biblical method for public identification. And they tend to deny the sovereignty of God.

But does this mean we stop evangelizing? Of course not. Consider Paul's example on Mars Hill in Acts 17. Here the apostle preached an articulate and doctrinally accurate message, calling people to repentance and emphasizing God's perfect judgment.

So how did his audience respond? Listen to Acts 17:32-34: "Now when they heard of the resurrection of the dead, some mocked. But others said, 'We will hear you again about this.' So Paul went out from their midst. But some men joined him and believed." The response to evangelism today still follows this threefold pattern. Some sneer and openly reject. Some are intrigued but not ready to commit. And some believe. Whenever the Word is preached, these are the varying responses that follow.

Again, our responsibility is not to coerce or manipulate those in the first two groups to join the third. Instead, we are called to faithfully preach the Word and leave the results to God. He will save His elect according to His own timing. If we are going to evangelize in a way that honors the Lord, we have to begin by trusting His sovereignty and relying on His Word.

Only after we are thoroughly convinced that God's Word is powerful enough to save (without added methods or techniques) will we be able to do away with the man-made altar call system. But when we do, we are able to see God work in people's lives without our manipulative interference. As a result, all of the glory goes to the Lord—and we can concentrate on being faithful in urgently inviting people to Christ rather than being numerically successful.

9

LET YOUR LIGHT SO SHINE: EXAMINING THE AMERICAN-CHRISTIAN APPROACH TO POLITICS

Phil Johnson

When it comes to volatile conversation starters, there are few topics as emotionally-charged as politics. After all, having a political opinion, along with the liberty to express that opinion, is part of what being American is all about. But how does that intersect with what being a Christian is all about? Are boycotts, bumper stickers, protests, and petitions vital (or even legitimate) instruments for Christian witness? Does God's Word support those who think the church ought to participate aggressively in the realm of secular politics? In this chapter, transcribed from a message given at Grace Community Church, Phil Johnson looks to a well-known Bible verse for answers to those questions.

Matthew 5:16 records Jesus' words, "let your light shine before others, so that they may see your good works and give glory to your Father who is in heaven." That's a simple verse, with a simple command, but there is nonetheless a lot of misunderstanding about what it means and what it demands of us. The passage and its context are often cited to justify evangelical activism in the political arena—as if this were Jesus' own rallying-call to get out the vote.

I recently heard someone on a nationally syndicated, evangelical radio broadcast trying to muster Christians for some political cause or another, urging believers to write their congressmen to protest this or that government policy, and he said, "We're *commanded* to be salt and light in our society, and that means we need to be a moral influence on our culture. The best way to do that is to use our collective clout in the voting booth. We need to make our voices heard, or we're not being salt and light the way Jesus commanded."

That view, and that interpretation of this passage, have become so commonplace nowadays that if you mention "salt and light" to the average evangelical congregation, they will probably assume you have some political agenda in mind.

But look at Matthew 5:16 carefully in its context, and you'll see that Jesus was not talking about political activism at all. This is not about mobilizing our clout as a voting bloc, organizing mass boycotts and protests, or electing Christians to public office. Jesus was calling for holy living at the individual level.

Now, please understand: I have no objection to Christians who run for political office. I have no doubt that God calls some of His people to serve in government, just as He calls some to serve in business, some to teach in universities, and others to work in every segment of society. All society is salted with Christians, and each one ought to have a beneficial effect in his circle of influence, no matter how big or small that circle may be. Collectively, we thereby enlighten, preserve, and season society as a whole. That truth is what this text is about.

But our influence as Christians is most effective at the personal, grassroots level. There's no suggestion in our text that the church's mission is to commandeer the apparatus of secular politics in order to wield our collective influence in society by legislative means. If you have the idea *that's* the best way (or the main way) the church is supposed to make her presence felt in secular society, you have missed the point of the text.

We ought to vote. We ought to be good citizens in every way. And we should cast our votes conscientiously and with discernment. But if your hope for the future of our society rests in the democratic process, or if you think the fortunes of the church rise or fall according to which party is in power, you need to look again at how the people of God have historically made their influence felt in society. You'll discover that those times when the church has grown the most and when revival has spread furthest are times when believers have been most concerned about personal holiness and evangelism. The church's real influence comes from the power of the gospel and the testimony of changed lives.

On the other hand, when influential Christians have tried to steer the church into the political process, their testimony has failed, and they have actually *lost* influence.

It's no wonder. In Matthew 20:25-28 Jesus says, "You know that the rulers of the Gentiles lord it over them, and their great ones exercise authority over them. It shall not be so among you. But whoever would be great among you must be your servant, and whoever would be first among you must be your slave, even as the Son of Man came not to be served but to serve, and to give his life as a ransom for many."

If the church is going to influence a hostile secular society like the one in which we live, political clout is *not* what we need. All the power, politics, and public policies in the world will never force unbelievers to yield their hearts to Christ as Lord.

And if you think that when Jesus described believers as salt and light He was calling His church to political activism, you need to look at this passage a little more closely.

Jesus is simply describing the natural, God-ordained process by which all of society is blessed and influenced by the presence of faithful believers who serve as salt and light in a corrupt and sin-darkened society. The key to it all is expressed in our verse. Namely, the more plentiful and visible our good works become, the more influence we have. *Personal holiness*, not *political dominion*, is what causes men to glorify our Father who is in heaven.

Look at verse 16 in its proper context. That verse is the culmination of a brief paragraph—verses 13-16—that comes immediately after the Beatitudes. This is part of the introduction to Jesus' Sermon on the Mount. He starts in verses 3-12 with the Beatitudes, a comprehensive list of blessings that highlight the true character of faith. He is pronouncing a formal blessing on the traits of authentic godliness.

What's most notable about the Beatitudes is that the qualities Jesus blesses are not the same attributes the world typically thinks are worthy of praise. *The world* glorifies power and dominion, force and physical strength, status and class. By contrast, *Jesus* blesses humility, meekness, mercy, mourning, purity of heart, and even persecution for righteousness' sake. Collectively, those things are the very opposite of political clout or partisan power. He's describing people who are willing to be oppressed and disenfranchised for the sake of true righteousness. They are peacemakers, not protestors; poor in spirit, not affluent and distinguished; people who are persecuted, not the pompous and the power-mongers.

Yet it is these poor and oppressed people whom Jesus is addressing when he says in verse 13, "You are the salt of the earth," and in verse 14, "You are the light of the world." He begins addressing them directly in verses 11-12: "Blessed are you when others revile you and persecute you and utter all kinds of evil against you falsely on my account. Rejoice and be glad, for your reward is great in heaven, for so they persecuted the prophets who were before you."

Whom is He speaking to? The believers in His audience, those who exemplified the traits He blessed in the Beatitudes—those who were persecuted for righteousness' sake, those who were reviled for His Name's sake. They were for the most part simple, common people—everyday folk from among "the crowds" (according to verse 1).

According to Mark 12:37, "the common people [were the ones who] heard him gladly" (KJV). He was not addressing the Sanhedrin (the spiritual rulers of Israel); nor was He talking to powerful men like Pilate, Herod, or Caiaphas. These "common people" did not have worldly influence like the Roman elite, or even a class of religious leaders like the Pharisees. And there is certainly no reason to think His audience consisted of political agitators like the Zealots. They were simple, common people who heard Him gladly. To *them* He said, "You are the salt of the earth. . . . You are the light of the world."

This was significant and probably shocking to the multitudes, because we know from the historical record that the title "light of the world" was an honor certain eminent rabbis liked to bestow on themselves. Spurgeon's comment on this passage is intriguing. He says:

> This title had been given by the Jews to certain of their eminent Rabbis. With great pomposity they spoke of Rabbi Judah, or Rabbi Jochanan, as the lamps of the universe, the lights of the world. It must have sounded strangely in the ears of the Scribes and Pharisees to hear that same title, in all soberness, applied to a few bronzed-faced and horny-handed peasants and fishermen, who had become disciples of Jesus. Jesus, in effect, said,—not the Rabbis, not the Scribes, not the assembled Sanhedrim, but ye, my humble followers, ye are the light of the world. He gave them this title, not after he had educated them for three years, but at almost the outset of his ministry; and from this I gather that the title was given them, not so much on account of what they knew, as on account of what they were. Not their knowledge, but their character made them the light of the world.[1]

Of course, Jesus also claimed that title for Himself in a very special and *unique* sense. It was one of His most explicit claims of deity. "I am the light of the world. Whoever follows me will not walk in darkness, but will have the light of life" (John 8:12). The apostle John explained the full significance of that claim at the very start of his Gospel, describing how the eternal Word of God, the Second Person of the Trinity, became flesh and dwelt among us. In 1:4-5 John writes, "In him was life, and the life was the light of men. The light shines in the darkness, and the darkness has not overcome it."

In other words (as John goes on to say in verse 9), Christ, "the true light, which enlightens everyone, was coming into the world."

He is the ultimate source of all light. He is like the sun, compared to which we are merely candles. And that's the imagery He uses here in Matthew 5:15. We are like candles—the light of the world in that limited sense, compared to Jesus, who is the Light of the world in a unique and infinitely greater sense.

But even as candles, we give off light, and even the faintest light of the smallest candle is capable of piercing and dispelling total darkness. The collective light of many candles has a still greater influence. That is how Jesus pictures our role in a sinful, dark, and fallen world.

Look briefly also at the metaphor of verse 13: "You are the salt of the earth, but if salt has lost its taste, how shall its saltiness be restored? It is no longer good for anything except to be thrown out and trampled under people's feet." Salt has several properties. Of course, it seasons and adds flavor. But what made salt most valuable in the world of the first century was that it acts as a preservative. Even raw meat could be cured and preserved with salt, so that it wouldn't spoil.

Christians in the midst of an evil and decaying society have a preserving and purifying effect. Remember in the days of Sodom that God told Abraham He would preserve the city from destruction for the sake of ten righteous people (see Gen 18). I'm convinced that even today God preserves societies from judgment for the sake of righteous people—the salt in their midst.

Salt also has an antiseptic property; so it was often used in the treatment of wounds. Of course, it hurts when you use it that way. Put salt on any type of open wound, and you'll instantly feel the sting of it. There seems to be an element of that idea in Jesus' metaphor. The presence of believers in the world irritates the consciences of the ungodly because it is a painful reminder that God requires holiness and that the wages of sin is death.

But salt also gives flavor to food and causes thirst—and I believe that's the main idea behind Christ's use of this metaphor, because He speaks of its flavor, its saltiness, its seasoning and taste-enhancing property, and its ability to magnify our thirst. Remember, Jesus had just blessed those who "hunger and thirst for righteousness" (v. 6), and this imagery suggests that the presence of godly people in society ought to have the natural effect of arousing an appetite and a thirst for righteousness.

"But," He says, "if salt has lost its taste, how shall its saltiness be restored?" If the salt goes flat, what do you season it with?

Now, scientifically we know that salt does not go flat. Salt is an element, and its saltiness is one of its inherent properties. It's not like other seasonings. A few years ago I bought one of those supersized containers of oregano, and I discovered it's not a good idea to buy most spices in bulk. Before I was able to use half of that oregano—after about five years in our cupboard—the oregano lost its flavor. Salt doesn't do that. You can leave it out for years, and it still has all the properties that make it salty.

So Jesus is giving a hypothetical situation here that is in reality impossible. Genuine salt—pure salt—doesn't lose its savor. If you sprinkle salt on your french fries and it's tasteless, it wasn't real salt to begin with; it was probably just sand. Some of the salt in the land of Israel wasn't pure salt. Most of it was gathered from around the Dead Sea, and it was hard to refine. It would get mixed with gypsum or otherwise diluted or contaminated, so that it sometimes tasted flat or had an unpleasant flavor. When you got a bad batch of salt, the only remedy was to throw it out. They understood exactly what He meant.

At this point Jesus switches metaphors. Now in addition to salt, He pictures believers as light. "You are the light of the world. A city set on a hill cannot be hidden. Nor do people light a lamp and put it under a basket, but on a stand, and it gives light to all in the house" (vv. 14-15).

You're like a bright light in a dark world, He says, and it's a misuse of light to keep it hidden. The purpose of light is to illuminate. The only reason to light a candle is to let it shine. You *can't* hide the light of a city that is properly situated, and you wouldn't want to light a candle and then cover it up. Doing so would be foolish and irrational.

And then He gives the command of our verse: "let your light shine before others, so that they may see your good works and give glory to your Father who is in heaven."

Notice something subtle but important: That is the only *command* in this passage. Jesus was not commanding His followers to *be* salt and light. You often hear people say that: "We're *commanded* to be salt and light." That's usually the argument given for why Christians ought to become political agitators. ("After all, we're *commanded* to be salt and light.")

But that's not the command that's given in this passage. Jesus is saying that if you are a true believer, you *are* salt and light. He's urging us not to lose our savor or hide our light. Salt is what it is by nature. Light is what it is by nature. You can contaminate salt or hide light, but you can't make sand into salt or turn a stone into a candle. So He doesn't "command" us to "be salt"; He says we *are* salt and cautions against losing our savor. He doesn't "command" us to be light; He says we *are* light and forbids us to hide under a bushel.

Notice what is supposed to happen when we let our light shine before men: They see our good works and glorify God. This is not about wielding political clout. It's not about organizing protests against ungodliness. It's not about trying to impose Christian values on society by legislation. It's about how we live, the testimony of our lives, the impact of the good works we do. It's about exemplifying the same traits Jesus blessed in the Beatitudes. That's how we let our light shine, and that's the saltiness we inject into an otherwise decaying and tasteless society.

I want to point out, by the way, that many evangelicals who have uncritically embraced the politics of the so-called religious right have exchanged the message of the gospel for a partisan political agenda. They have actually thrown out the savory salt and bought gypsum instead. Listen to their message and it's all about the next election, the latest piece of legislation, or the current pending moral crisis in secular society. You *won't* often hear them preach Christ, because the unadulterated message of the gospel is an offense to some of their political allies.

Remember, Christ is the only true light of the world, and you and I cannot be candles to illuminate the darkness of this world if we have to stifle our testimony for Christ in order to advance some partisan political agenda. Even if we're working for a valid moral cause, if we have to hide the only true light we possess in order to court political allies, then we're simply not obeying Christ's command in this passage.

He's calling us to stand out in this world—to be different. More than that, He's saying we *are* different, because He has made us something different, and we should embrace what we are. We're salt in a decaying and tasteless culture, and we're light in a dark world. If we give up (or cover up) what makes us distinctive, we lose our savor and forfeit our only real influence. If we have to squelch the heart of the message Christ has called us to proclaim, we're guilty of hiding our light under a bushel. Those who think the church can have a greater influence by adopting a worldly strategy are actually undermining the only valid influence Christians can have on society.

When we merely imitate the world by jumping on every secular bandwagon, or when we make worldly alliances to advance political causes, or when we adopt worldly strategies to win the world's approval, we forfeit our distinctiveness. It's my conviction that much of the modern evangelical movement is guilty of that kind of compromise. We've put sand instead of salt in the saltshaker, and we've put a bushel basket over our candle.

Here's the remedy: "Let your light shine before others, so that they may see your good works and give glory to your Father who is in heaven." This speaks to us on an individual, as well as a collective, level. It describes what we must do corporately as a church; it gives a much-needed corporate corrective to the evangelical movement as a whole. But notice, it also reveals what you and I need to be doing as individuals.

Do you want your life to count for eternity? Do you want to maximize the influence of your life on your children, your neighbors, the people at work, people in your community, and ultimately the whole world? Here is *Jesus'* strategy for spreading the light, one candle at a time. This is what He calls you and me to do: "Let your light shine before others, so that they may see your good works and give glory to your Father who is in heaven."

Now, think about what the imagery of this statement means: *Light* speaks of our testimony for Christ. If Christ is the only "true light" as John 1:9 suggests, then I can't let *my* light shine unless my life and my words testify about Christ. And the more I testify about Christ, the brighter my light shines.

Some have suggested that Jesus' only emphasis here is on the testimony of our behavior, because the verse specifically mentions "good works," which is what people are supposed to see, and that is what provokes them to glorify God. But surely Jesus is not excluding the testimony of our words as well. I'm reminded of Paul's words in Romans 10:9: "if you confess with your mouth that Jesus is Lord and believe in your heart that God raised him from the dead, you will be saved."

You aren't really a faithful follower of Christ if you won't confess Him with your mouth. I know many people advocate a kind of silent evangelism. They think if you live a good enough life, people will see Christ in your behavior, and by the sheer power of your example, sinners will be drawn to Him, even if you never mention His name.

But that's not what Scripture teaches, either by precept or by example. If your lips are silent about Christ, then you're not faithfully letting your light shine before men the way Christ intended. You need to confess Him with your mouth. You need to proclaim the gospel with your lips. Remember that "it pleased God through the folly of what we preach to save those who believe" (1 Cor 1:21). After all, "faith comes from hearing, and hearing through the word of Christ" (Rom 10:17); and "how are they to hear without someone preaching?" (Rom 10:14). The gospel, not the silent witness of your good works, is the power of God unto salvation.

In other words, you're called to proclaim the gospel with your words. Confess Christ with your mouth. Speak to people about Him. Proclaim the message of the gospel. This is the very heart and an essential aspect of what Jesus means when He says, "Let your light shine."

In fact, it is only as we let our light shine through our *words* that people can see our *good works* in the true light. That's the only way they can understand *why* all the good works you and I do are to the praise and glory of God alone. If we never spoke of Christ and never confessed our own unworthiness, why would anyone who sees our good works glorify *God?* They'd be more inclined to elevate us instead. But as we shine the light by proclaiming the gospel, we confess our own sinfulness, we point to the grace of God in Christ, and we therefore give glory to God, where all glory rightfully belongs.

Now, of course, the verse *does* speak of "good works," and it reminds us that they are a vital part of our testimony to the world. On the one hand, you can't be a good testimony for Christ through your works apart from your words. But the opposite is true as well, and it also needs to be said: You aren't a good testimony for Christ if your walk doesn't match your talk. There are always a few misguided souls who think extra zeal in preaching the gospel makes up for a glaring lack of holiness, personal discipline, kindness, or love. That misses the whole point. "Let your light so shine before others, so that they may see your *good works.*" If your life is devoid of any distinctive goodness, then change your behavior before you openly tarnish the name of Christ.

MATTHEW 5:16 AND THE CHRISTIAN'S PERSPECTIVE

With the context of this verse in mind, consider what is involved in our calling to be lights to the world. Instead of centering on political agendas or selfish pursuits, Matthew 5:16 presents us with both the right motivation and the right means for impacting culture. Here are three reasons we need to understand our duty as light-bearers in a dark world.

1. It Gives Us a Proper Perspective on Self

It is the natural tendency of every fallen heart to be selfish, self-centered, and self-absorbed. We tend to see ourselves as the center of the universe. Our fallen flesh would even seek a way, if possible, to make holiness itself a self-aggrandizing, pride-inducing hobby. That's exactly what the Pharisees did. Jesus says in Matthew 6:5 that hypocrites "love to stand and pray in the synagogues and at the street corners, that they may be seen by others." In Matthew 23:5-7 He said, "They do all their deeds to be seen by others. For they make their phylacteries broad and their fringes long, and they love the place of honor at feasts and the best seats in the synagogues and greetings in the marketplaces and being called rabbi by others."

In fact, look at the beginning of Matthew 6. This is the very thing Jesus cautions against. "Beware of practicing your righteousness before other people in order to be seen by them, for then you will have no reward from your Father who is in heaven" (v. 1). He reiterates this in verse 2, when He commands His followers not to sound a trumpet before giving alms. In verses 3-4 He continues: "But when you give to the needy, do not let your left hand know what your right hand is doing, so that your giving may be in secret. And your Father who sees in secret will reward you." Verse 6 goes one step farther: "But when you pray, go into your room and shut the door and pray to your Father who is in secret. And your Father who sees in secret will reward you." Even fasting is included in verses 17-18: "But when you fast, anoint your head and wash your face, that your fasting may not be seen by others but by your Father who is in secret. And your Father who sees in secret will reward you."

So how do those commands (requiring us to perform certain religious acts in secret) relate to Matthew 5:16: "Let your light shine before others, so that they may see your good works and give glory to your Father who is in heaven"? Is Jesus contradicting Himself? Of course not. In chapter 6 he's talking about acts of private devotion and worship—the kind of good works that are between the worshiper and God and therefore don't need to be done publicly. But in Matthew 5 He's talking about the kind of good works that reflect the qualities of the Beatitudes. These are good works done for the benefit of others and not for self.

And that's the key. It goes to motive. What Christ *commends* are selfless acts done to serve others. What He *forbids* are selfish or self-righteous acts done purely for show or for the exaltation of self. A proper understanding of our text is a good antidote to selfishness and spiritual pride. It's a reminder that the only *truly* good works are the ones done with the other person's interests in mind. In this case, it's speaking of good works done for the benefit of those still in the bondage of darkness and confusion.

This command helps us keep that perspective. It's a clear reminder that Christ hasn't called anyone to be a monk or an ascetic. You can't achieve Christlike holiness by moving into a cave or locking yourself in an ivory tower.

Some Christians practically sever all relationships with unbelievers and try to isolate themselves and their children in a Christian bubble. But Christ reminds us that He has left us in this world to be lights, not to hide in a closet or under a bushel. We are to light the way for the unbelieving people of the world. We can't do that by locking ourselves away permanently in a secret enclave or by living behind walls in a Christian commune.

Here's what Paul said to the Corinthians in 1 Corinthians 5:9: "I wrote you in my letter not to associate with sexually immoral people." *Aha!* you say. *Paul doesn't want us to have fellowship with wicked people!* No, listen:

> *I wrote to you in my letter not to associate with sexually immoral people—not at all meaning the sexually immoral of this world, or the greedy and swindlers, or idolaters, since then you would need to go out of the world. But now I am writing to you not to associate with anyone who bears the name of brother if he is guilty of sexual immorality or greed, or is an idolater, reviler, drunkard, or swindler—not even to eat with such a one. (vv. 9-11)*

We're not of this world, but Christ has left us *in* it for a reason. It's not a selfish reason. It's so we can be shining lights for the benefit of others who are still in bondage to sin. We're not to be conformed to this world, and that is part of Jesus' message here as well. (We're to be distinctive and different—savory and bright.) But while we're in this world, we are here for the benefit of others. When we embrace that duty, it serves as an antidote to our own sinful self-centeredness.

2. It Gives Us a Proper Perspective on Our Neighbors

Not only does this verse change the way we view ourselves, it also impacts the way we view our unbelieving neighbors. In fact, one of the greatest dangers inherent in the political activism of the so-called religious right is that it fosters a tendency to make enemies out of people who are supposed to be our mission field, even while we're forming political alliances with Pharisees and false teachers.

In fact, before I became a Christian I was a political zealot. That was back in the sixties and the early seventies when it seemed the whole student world supported left-wing politics. But I was different. I was a conservative. And some of my closest friends and political allies were evangelical Christians who were part of the religious right—even before Jerry Falwell and James Dobson brought conservative politics into the mainstream of the evangelical movement.

When I finally understood the gospel and came to Christ, it was not because any of my politically-active Christian friends explained the gospel to me. They would never have done that, for fear they would alienate a political ally. But I have to say, I felt a sense of betrayal when I finally understood the gospel and realized that some of my born-again friends had never once talked to me about the state of my soul. That's the danger of being obsessed with politics and thinking the church's agenda can be advanced through political means: You quickly lose sight of the real mission.

To hear some Christians today talk, you might think that rampant sins like homosexuality and abortion in America can be solved by legislation. A hundred years ago the pet issue was prohibition, and mainstream evangelicalism embraced the notion that outlawing liquor in America would solve the problem of drunkenness forever. It was a waste of time and energy, and I believe it was an unhealthy diversion for many in the church. Listen to Paul: "If righteousness comes through the Law, then Christ died needlessly" (Gal 2:21,

NASB). "If a law had been given that could give life, then righteousness would indeed be by the law" (Gal 3:21).

We have the true and only answer to sins like homosexuality,
divorce, drug addiction, and other forms of rampant immorality. It's
the glorious liberty of salvation in Christ. It's a message about the
grace of God, which has accomplished what no law could ever do.
And we need to proclaim that message, befriending our neighbors,
not taking a hostile stance against them, but letting the light of the
glorious gospel of Christ shine unto them.

We're like lighthouse keepers in a dark and stormy world. We've
been given a mission of rescue and mercy toward sinners. We can't
be like James and John, who in a moment of weakness and immatu-
rity wanted to call down fire from heaven to destroy sinners. We are
ambassadors of the true light, who came down to earth to seek and
to save the lost. "God did not send his Son into the world to condemn
the world, but in order that the world might be saved through him"
(John 3:17).

There's a true sense in which we are not to love the world or the
things of the world. But the *people* of the world are another matter.
We're supposed to love them all, including our enemies. Scripture is
clear on this. We don't condone sin, and we certainly can't pretend to
let our lights shine if we're having fellowship with darkness. But we
should have a Christlike love for sinners. It is an essential part of what
He demands when He calls us to let our lights shine, so that people
see our good works and glorify our heavenly Father. In this way, true
disciples of Christ must be markedly different from the Pharisees.

If we don't have a sense of deep compassion and heartfelt benev-
olence toward sinners, we're not letting our light shine. We are
redeemed sinners, and to look on other sinners with disgust is inex-
cusable pride. That was the very sin of the Pharisee in Luke 18:11,
who "standing by himself, prayed thus: 'God, I thank you that I am
not like other men, extortioners, unjust, adulterers, or even like this
tax collector.'" Jesus said that attitude is what kept this Pharisee from
being justified in God's eyes. Jesus, by contrast, "when he saw the
crowds . . . had compassion for them, because they were harassed and

helpless, like sheep without a shepherd" (Matt 9:36). That's the perspective you'll have if you embrace Jesus' command to be a light to the world.

Remember, this is how Christ says our influence becomes most powerful in a sin-darkened world. It's not by our words only, and not by our deeds only, but by the faithful proclamation of the gospel, accompanied by good works of mercy and love and compassion toward even our enemies.

That is what Christ said would cause the world to take notice of the truth and glorify God. Embrace that duty and you'll gain a whole new perspective on your neighbors.

3. It Gives Us a Proper Perspective on Human Responsibility

A third benefit found in Matthew 5:16 is this: By embracing our role as lights in this world, we gain a proper perspective on our responsibility—especially our duty as evangelists. Matthew 5:16 compels us to be faithful witnesses and obliterates any excuse to be anything less.

This verse is a clear antidote to hyper-Calvinistic fatalism. Don't imagine for a moment that the doctrine of divine sovereignty is an excuse for apathy or inactivity when it comes to the task of winning people to Christ. Let me quote Spurgeon one more time. He said,

> God's decrees shall be fulfilled. There are, however, persons who argue from this, that therefore we may sit down and do nothing as to the salvation of others. Such persons are very foolish, because they must be aware that the same logic which would drive them to do nothing spiritually would require them to do nothing in other matters, so that they would neither eat, nor drink, nor think, nor breathe, do nothing, in fact, but lie like logs, passive under fate's iron sway. That is too absurd to need an answer. Believers are cured of that tendency by the belief that they are the lights of the world.[2]

We're given *work* to do. This text lays a responsibility on us. We're called to be evangelists. We become instruments in the hands of a sovereign God for the salvation of others as we obey the command of this text. We can't be idle. Those who would use God's sovereignty as an excuse for apathy or indifference have corrupted sound doctrine. This is Christ Himself commanding us to let our lights so shine before men that they see our good works and glorify God.

It's a weighty responsibility, isn't it? There is a true sense in which the eternal destiny of men depends on what we do, because God has chosen us to be the instruments of light to show the way. And if you hide your light under a bushel, you will not be able to plead the doctrine of God's sovereignty as an excuse before the judgment seat of Christ.

But this command is a corrective not only for hyper-Calvinists and fatalists—it's also a rebuke to halfhearted people who squander their time and their earthly resources on entertainment and other selfish pursuits. Granted, there's nothing wrong with a modest amount of relaxation and leisure in this life. God made us with a need for rest and recreation, and Christ recognized that need by taking His own disciples away from the rigors of public ministry for times of pure rest and refreshment. Scripture says in 1 Timothy 6:17 that "God . . . richly provides us with everything to enjoy."

But that's not the main point of life, and we need to resist the temptation—especially in a pleasure-addicted society like ours—to make entertainment and amusement the center and the focus of our spare time.

We have a duty, a God-given responsibility (and it's a serious and solemn responsibility), to shine as bright lights in a dark world, proclaiming Christ to a lost world and doing good works that provoke and persuade people to honor our heavenly Father.

How brightly is *your* light shining? What kind of response does your life provoke from your unsaved neighbors? Are your good works the kind that glorify God, or are they the self-righteous works of a Pharisee? Is your testimony an instrument God could use to draw hostile sinners to Himself?

Clearly, we all have some work to do. We live in a world that is perishing for lack of knowledge. How will they hear the good news unless we tell them? And why would they listen unless our lives are consistent with our message?

On the other hand, if we obey the simple command of Matthew 5:16, we *will* begin to make a profound difference in the world, both individually and collectively. In the words of the apostle Paul in Philippians 2:15-16, we can be—and we *must* be—"blameless and innocent, children of God without blemish in the midst of a crooked and twisted generation, among whom you shine as lights in the world, holding fast to the word of life." Only then will we truly make a difference in our society.

10

CHOKING ON CHOICES: COMBATING CONSUMERISM WITH A BIBLICAL MIND-SET

Kurt Gebhards

This chapter addresses the consumer mentality that has invaded contemporary Christianity. To clarify, the chapter is not a challenge to swelling credit card debt or shrinking offering plates, overdressed parishioners or underpaid pastors. In fact, it is not primarily about money, but rather about the heart of the worshiper. Sadly, marketplace consumerism has been imported into God's church as Christians enjoy the power of product choice. Because they fail to discern what is truly valuable, too many Christians are exchanging eternal riches for temporal pursuits. This chapter calls the church back to a clear perspective as the devastating effects of Christian consumerism are explored.

Americans in the twenty-first century are the consummate consumers—a fact that became clear to me some years ago on a ministry trip to Russia. While there, I experienced a radical cross-cultural event when I walked into a Russian "supermarket." As I stepped inside, I immediately noticed the grocery section of the store. By American standards it was tiny—consisting of only two bookshelf-sized racks. All the food in the entire store was on those two shelves. Where are all the choices? Where is the selection? I wondered, thinking back to the supermarkets where I normally shopped. As an American-grown consumer, this was certainly not what I was used to, with the options limited to a bare minimum.

Recently I decided to compare what I found in Russia with the typical American grocery store. So, on a routine shopping trip I counted the number of choices for various products. There were 264 breakfast cereal options—name brand and generic; mega-pack, large, medium, small, and single-serving boxes; puffy, crunchy, and sugary; healthy and high-fiber. I also counted sixty-two different containers of mustard, 305 deodorant choices, and 198 varieties of toothbrushes.

What a contrast this was to the two shelves of groceries I had seen overseas—a comparison that highlighted for me just how pervasive the consumer mentality is in American culture. It is a mind-set that cherishes the opportunity to choose, a mind-set that expects to be served as the consumer. From food to furniture, from clothes to cars, we naturally favor the products that please us most and the people who treat us best. "Customer first" is more than just good business policy—it is a slogan that characterizes what American capitalism has come to expect.

Sadly, many American Christians carry this attitude from the marketplace into the church. As a result, they view themselves as "customers" in search of a religious product that can meet their felt needs and fulfill their desires. Instead of seeing themselves as servants, they regard the church as a place to be accommodated and served. Rather than being God-focused, they are self-focused. Rather than acknowledging the church as a place where God is the "customer," they see themselves as the center of attention, expecting their wants to be fulfilled. In a day that is monopolized by materialism, I believe this attitude of consumerism is one of the American church's greatest idols.

The choices we enjoy in a grocery store certainly speak to God's wonderful abundance. However, problems arise when Christians approach church with the same consumer mentality. While we may select a certain brand or flavor based on the whims of fancy, we must be careful not to be so capricious when committing ourselves to a certain church or ministry. Yet I am convinced that for some church-shoppers there is little difference between how they approach each of these two decisions.

While I am not arguing that we shouldn't have any choice, I am arguing that it is unwise to make that choice sovereign. In other words, we must submit our choices to the commands of God. We all have preferences, but we have to remember, as believers, that God's Word overrides our wants and our desires. The goal of this chapter, then, is to help choice-saturated, capitalistic, American Christians discern the difference between seeking God's kingdom and building their own.

WHAT IS CHRISTIAN CONSUMERISM?

At its core, consumerism is *me-ism*—calling us to exalt ourselves as the arbiter of all our affairs. Daily we are encouraged to choose everything from our clothing to our coffee in keeping with our personal desires. Preference is given ultimate priority. As a result, we begin to believe the myth that life is all about us and what we want. Perhaps that is what makes shopping such a solace. When things are tough and trials come, we enter the marketplace and become credit card kings for an afternoon. And when this attitude spills over into what we look for in a church, we have a serious problem on our hands.

Instead of shopping for a church that fits our criteria, our desire, as God's servants, should be to find a ministry that meets His standards. The question should not be, "Are *my* expectations met?" but rather, "Are *God's* expectations met?" In spite of the market-driven culture around us, we should work hard to root out the self-centered perspective that American materialism breeds. Ultimately we must each ask ourselves, "As we come to God's house, what weighs more heavily on our hearts—His expectations for sacrificial service and worship, or our own expectations for personal fulfillment?"

It must be remembered that God is the rightful focus of corporate worship, not the Christian. And God has certain expectations. He expects us to faithfully participate at church; He expects us to bring a premeditated offering of praise to Him; He expects us to be zealous and passionate for Him; He expects us to be cheerfully committed to His purposes; He expects us to eagerly anticipate the teaching of His Word; and He expects us to prepare our bodies and minds to enter into the King's court.

WHAT CAUSES CHRISTIAN CONSUMERISM?

Without question, human beings are naturally attracted to the consumer mind-set. But why is that the case? What are the influences that contribute to consumerism? I believe the answer to this question is twofold.

First, there are cultural forces that contribute to the consumer mind-set. These forces include humanism, philosophical existentialism, and modern materialism. Humanism forms the foundation—looking admiringly upon the human race (and the individual) in order to appreciate human capacity and worth. Humanism legitimizes our heart's self-centered desires, giving them credibility. Existentialism argues that the key to all existence is essence. In practice, this means that personal experience, feeling, and satisfaction is what life is all about. Existentialism gives freedom to our heart's desires to express themselves fully and without constraint. Finally, materialism appeals to our humanistic and existential desires, cultivating a mind-set that looks for personal benefit in all things. As a result, we are told that our choice, as the consumer, is sovereign.

In addition to these cultural forces, there are also carnal factors that contribute to the consumer mentality. These include spiritual ignorance, pride, and apathy. Spiritual ignorance, for example, forgets the priority of God (Rom 11:36; Col 1:18)—simultaneously resulting in a perilously low view of His church. Consequently, many

Christians see church attendance as optional, church membership as unnecessary, and church authority as unimportant. Spiritual pride complicates matters by convincing Christians that their wishes are more important than God's prerogatives. This rebellious attitude evidences itself when people choose churches for the wrong reasons. "I am the captain of my own ship!" they shout defiantly. Finally, spiritual apathy leads to an overall indifference for God's glory. This lack of passion for the greatness of God severely inhibits any ability to overcome attitudes of self-centeredness. The snare of Christian consumerism can only be evaded by rooting out these carnal forces, along with their cultural counterparts.

WHAT CHARACTERIZES CHRISTIAN CONSUMERISM?

So how do these forces manifest themselves in the church? What are the specific evidences of Christian consumerism? Allow me to highlight three attitudes that reflect a consumerist mentality.

1. *Self-focused egotism.* Self-focus displaces God from His throne in the church. For the egotistical consumer the orientation is no longer God but self. The consumer asks, "What do I get out of this? Are my expectations met? What's in it for me?" In his heart, self-pleasure is exalted and God is dethroned. Divine approval is exchanged for what pleases the customer.

Haggai 1 is a passage of tremendous insight on this topic—especially because the parallels between the early exilic period in Israel and the modern evangelical movement in America are striking. The Jewish exiles had returned from Babylon in 536 B.C. and had begun the rebuilding of the temple under the leadership of Zerrubabel (Ezra 6:1-22). However, the efforts to rebuild God's house were short-lived. Within two years the work had stopped. Why? The Jews had become distracted with their own homes, wanting to live in comfort and luxury. As a result, they forgot about finishing the Lord's house. After fourteen years of patient waiting, God sent Haggai to confront the Jews because they had supplanted God's expectations with their own desires. They concentrated on their homes while God Himself remained homeless (Hag 1:9).

Another prophet, Malachi, also confronted this same spirit of self-focused egotism. In Malachi 1:6, 9-10, the text reflects an aston-ishing reversal in worship. Listen to the Lord's rebuke:

> "A son honors his father, and a servant his master. If then I am a father, where is my honor? And if I am a master, where is my fear? says the LORD of hosts to you, O priests, who despise my name. But you say, 'How have we despised your name?' . . . And now entreat the favor of God, that he may be gracious to us. With such a gift from your hand, will he show favor to any of you? says the LORD of hosts. Oh that there were one among you who would shut the doors, that you might not kin-dle fire on my altar in vain! I have no pleasure in you, says the LORD of hosts, and I will not accept an offering from your hand."

God was looking for the honor and respect that was due Him. He arrived in His temple expecting to be the Master, and He had been unseated; He arrived in the temple expecting the veneration due a father. Instead He was disgraced.

What had happened? The Jews had made themselves the masters. They had stolen glory and reverence from God such that when God looked, there was none for Him. In the same way, we exalt ourselves when we seek to pursue our desires rather than pursuing His. Clearly, God seeks honor from us as our Father and Master. He expects to be significant and weighty to us. Praise is His rightful possession. As the Father and Lord of His people, He deserves our reverence and wor-ship, especially in the very place specifically designated for such. Yet many believers fail to give Him the honor He is due.

This self-focused self-exaltation is at the heart of Christian con-sumerism, which is why it denigrates God. Consumerism puts God *below* the base level of our preferences and renders His purposes sub-servient to our desires. Consumerism prioritizes our opinions above the God of the universe and dramatically reverses right priorities.

Along these lines, Steven Charnock extends a warning in his book
The Existence and Attributes of God:

> When we believe that we should be satisfied, rather than that God
> should be glorified, we put God below ourselves as though He
> has been made for us, not we for Him. There is no greater blas-
> phemy than using God as our servant and there is no worse place
> to do it than the realm of worship where we make the worship of
> God to end in ourselves rather than in God.

How is self-focused egotism evidenced in the contemporary
church? The consumer in the church looks for what he will *get* from
church rather than what he can *give* to God. He makes comments
like, "I will *get* inspiration and encouragement," "I will *get* knowledge
and instruction," "I will *get* a boost to last me through the week," "I
will *get* a blessing," "I will *get* new friends." By focusing on his own
felt needs, the Christian consumer misses the whole point of worship—namely, God.

At its root, Christian consumerism is the old-fashioned sin of
idolatry, because it brings false worship (self-worship) into the house
of God. As a result,

> Our services are often celebrations of ourselves more than they
> are of God. Never before, not even in the Medieval Church, have
> Christians been so obsessed with themselves. Self-esteem, self-
> confidence, self-this, self-that have replaced talk of God's
> attributes. Ironically, it has created the opposite of its intention.
> Without the knowledge of God in whose image we have been cre-
> ated and the grace which has made us the children of God, nar-
> cissism, or self-love, quickly evolves into depression.[1]

In other words, it is spiritual tail-chasing for any believer to
attempt personal fulfillment in a biblical church. God's house is
erected for His glory and the fulfillment of His purposes. Lives that
glorify Him in worship and holiness are lives filled with grace and

peace, but those blessings are secondary, resulting from a God-glorifying focus.

For those who refuse to worship God, staying centered on themselves instead, the consequences are devastating. The Christian consumer makes God his enemy, because God is jealous for His glory (Exod 34:14). In Malachi 2:2, for example, God offers a severe warning:

> *If you will not listen, if you will not take it to heart to give honor to my name, says the LORD of hosts, then I will send the curse upon you and I will curse your blessings.*

Christians who think the church is here to serve them should stop, take heed, and repent.

2. *Self-styled pragmatism.* In addition to self-centered egotism, Christian consumerism also manifests itself through self-styled pragmatism—an attitude that seeks to serve God on its own terms and in its own wisdom. Self-styled believers serve God as *they* see fit. They are not motivated by God's glory, nor do they feel compelled to honor His commands. Their Christian practice is according to their own preconceived notions rather than the objective parameters of Scripture.

Self-styled pragmatism often maintains the outward appearance of godliness. Unlike self-focused egotism, it is not *overtly* self-seeking. Instead the pragmatist seeks to be involved as long as the involvement is according to his terms and for his glory.

The self-styled pragmatist is also mentioned in Malachi 1. After God confronts the Jews for stealing His glory and honor, He challenges them for bringing Him substandard offerings. The people had entered God's courts on their own terms. They had brought sacrifices that were acceptable in their own eyes, without regard for God's expectations or requirements. In essence, they were holding to a "have it your way" form of religion. But God was not impressed. Listen to His perspective in verses 7-8:

"[You are] offering polluted food upon my altar. But you say, "How have we polluted you?" By saying that the LORD's table may be despised. When you offer blind animals in sacrifice, is that not evil? And when you offer those that are lame or sick, is that not evil? Present that to your governor; will he accept you or show you favor?"

Instead of honoring the Lord, they defiled His altar with unqualified offerings. They tried to draw near to God with defiled sacrifices, rotten fruit, and crippled animals. In the process, their attempts to honor God only denigrated His temple (v. 12). They may have paid homage to God with their lips, but they were unwilling to do the same with their lives.

As Christians, living 2,500 years later, we must be careful not to repeat this mistake. Our desire should be to bring an offering that is pleasing and acceptable to God. Like the Old Testament sacrifices—which were to be perfect (Lev 22:20; Mal 1:11) and without blemish (Exod 12:5; 29:1)—so should our praise be. Nothing should ever be offered to God that is not worthy of His approval.

A self-styled approach to worship is repulsive to God. When people with this attitude enter the church, God moves out. God demands more than the mere performance of His commands. He expects that we do *what* He wants, the *way* He wants, and with a *heart motive* that glorifies Him.

A distinguishing characteristic of the self-styled pragmatist is a lack of fervent worship. True worship is a full-hearted expression of the greatness of God. But self-styled worship lacks heart-felt passion and zeal. Warren Wiersbe responds to such artificial attempts at praise:

> If we look upon worship only as a means of getting something from God rather than giving something to God, then we make God our servant instead of our Lord and the elements of worship become a cheap formula for selfish gratification. When worship becomes pragmatic, it ceases to be worship.

When God is belittled, there remains no room for worship. If

God is torn down, there is nothing left to worship except self.
Christian consumerism simply cannot coexist with a true and pure
worship of God.

In recent years a dramatic change has occurred within the church
concerning worship. What would have seemed impossible a generation ago is almost a universal reality. Once the church was a place for
those seeking transcendent help, eager to consider God as the reference point. Today, however, the church is a place of self-indulgence
and self-satisfaction. Self-interest has become pandemic, even in
worship, making it difficult for some churchgoers to imagine that
Christianity is not intended to revolve around them.

Not long ago I was watching a Christian concert on television.
There were thirty singers on a stage with a few pianos. The host was
circulating throughout the musicians with a microphone and asked
one of the singers for a "testimony." She told a story of how God
delivered her from a trial. After hearing her account, the program's
host became excited and said, "I am not quite sure where this is in the
Bible, maybe you scholars know, but the Word says that if we worship God He will set up ambushments for our enemies.
Ambushments! Ambushments! Can you believe that if we sing and
worship, God will set up ambushments for those who want to
ambush us? Ambushments! Ambushments!"

Aside from a unique use of English, the host radically redefined
worship, turning it on its head. He made worship man-centered—
suggesting that worship's value is found in the fact that God helps us.
But this thoroughly misrepresents and misunderstands the nature of
true praise. Worship must be about God, and not about us. And it
must be conducted on His terms, not ours.

3. Self-absorbed individualism. A third manifestation of Christian
consumerism is self-absorbed individualism—an attitude that
demands independence and seeks to be left alone. The self-absorbed
Christian is a *solo lobo* (lone wolf), a *lone ranger*, and a *maverick*. As
much as possible, the authority of the church is disregarded, account-
ability is avoided, and personal participation is sidestepped. While he

might be a regular attendee, he shies away from any formal connection or commitment to the ministry.

The attitude of the self-absorbed Christian reminds me of Narcissus, a character from Greek mythology. According to the myth, Narcissus was the most handsome mortal man whom the gods made. He loved himself so much and was so fond of his own good looks that he never found a suitable mate. But one day, when bending over a still pool of water, he mistook his reflection for a beautiful nymph. Immediately he fell in love, and he decided to wait until the nymph came out of the pool. Of course, the nymph never emerged, and Narcissus died there in love with himself.

It is this same type of self-love that characterizes the self-absorbed individualist. He finds in himself all the ability and adequacy he thinks he needs. He avoids scrutiny and rejects any spiritual input from the body of Christ. In his mind, he has no need for others. As a consumer, he takes only what he wants to take, rejecting everything else as unnecessary to his own self-sufficiency.

But this mind-set is certainly not biblical. Proverbs 18:1 gives this warning: "Whoever isolates himself seeks his own desire; he breaks out against all sound judgment." Human beings were not designed to live alone. They were made to live in community. Nowhere in Scripture do we find long periods of isolation commended or exemplified. Rather, the New Testament pictures the church as a body of multiple parts, a building of multiple stones, a flock of multiple sheep, a vine of multiple branches, and so on. Like hot coals, we need one another if we are to continue burning brightly for the cause of Christ. It's no wonder that the author of Hebrews commands us to not forsake congregational worship and fellowship (Heb 10:25). In fact, we are to be absorbed with Christ (cf. Phil 1:21) and concerned with the needs of others (cf. Phil 2:1-4). This is exactly the opposite of self-absorbed individualism (cf. 1 Cor 11:17-22).

The mind-set that allows sinful desires to reign unabated cannot coexist with God's expectation of humble service in the church. Service is the antithesis of consumerism. The difficulty with consumerism is that he who reigns as king in the marketplace finds it hard to cast himself as a servant in the ministry place. Yet, this is exactly what Christ call us to: "If anyone would be first, he must be last of all and servant of all" (Mark 9:35).

WHAT COUNTERACTS CHRISTIAN CONSUMERISM?

The doctrine of the church has reached a definite low point in our generation. Its authority has been almost completely eroded, and its expectations have often been minimized as biblical standards are ignored. In addition, some Christians—like the founders of the relatively new Emergent Church—argue that the church's primary purpose actually is the exaltation of self. In contrast, God's Word condemns such manifestations of Christian consumerism, mandating that we pursue God's esteem rather than self-esteem. So how can we cultivate a right view of ourselves? How can we eliminate an attitude of Christian consumerism?

First, *commit to biblical introspection.* We are challenged in Scripture to distrust our inclinations and to test ourselves (2 Cor 13:5) in order that we might have a biblical view of ourselves and our sin. With the help of the Holy Spirit (John 4:23), believers who have lived under the delusions of a consumer mind-set can recognize their wrong thinking and repent. But this begins with allowing God's Word to penetrate our lives and convict us of our shortcomings (cf. Heb 4:12).

Second, *root out the selfishness in your life.* Transform all self-centered perspectives into God-centered purposes. Since we are naturally selfish and seek personal benefit in all things, a deity who is primarily interested in *His own* glory, rather than our benefit, may initially seem oppressive and cruel. But this is simply not the case, for we can never find true fulfillment and satisfaction until we find it wholly in Him and His will. We are at our best when we selflessly worship our great God.

Third, *submit gladly to God's expectations.* Realize that He makes demands on your life. His expectations are established in the Word of God; we are to honor and obey them. We must remind ourselves that Christ is both our Savior *and* Lord (Rom 10:9-10). As His servants, we must embrace the service to which He calls us.

Fourth, *live for worship*. A life of sincere worship is a sure antidote for consumerism—because by definition worship takes our eyes off ourselves and directs them heavenward. As we focus on Jesus Christ (cf. Col 3:1-2), we will find our lives consumed with His passions and desires rather than our own preferences. This, of course, is the antithesis of consumerism. In the same way that it is impossible to travel east and west at the same time, it is impossible to simultaneously serve both self and God (cf. Matt 6:24).

CONCLUSION

Our Christian culture has become so saturated with a consumer mind-set that such self-centeredness is no longer perceived as a vice. The poison of pride, coupled with a perilously inadequate view of God and His church, beckons twenty-first-century believers to promote their own self-worth. The result is a church full of egotistical, pragmatic, and individualistic Christians who are more interested in serving themselves than in serving God. But the Bible calls us to do just the opposite—to deny ourselves (cf. Mark 8:34).

While self-worship erodes the work of the church, God still seeks true worshipers to build His church (John 4:24). This chapter is offered in the hopes that we might experience a tide-reversal in our day. Our prayer is that the church would enjoy a renewed passion to serve God, love Him, and make Him everything. Let us usher in a new trend of God-honoring worship that places Him in His rightful place and us in ours (cf. Eccles 5:1-2). Let us offer ourselves on the altar of true worship, putting our own preferences aside for the sake of His kingdom and His glory (Rom 12:1-2).

PART FOUR

Pursuing Discernment in Your Daily Life

11

HILLⱲ TO DIE ON: A DOCTRINAL FRAMEWORK FOR DEVELOPING DIⱤCERNMENT

Dan Dumas

Having explored the need for biblical discernment—and having applied it to several practical issues—this chapter lays the groundwork for how a Christian can develop discernment in his or her own life. Rather than always depending on the opinions of others, every Christian should develop the ability to think rightly about spiritual matters. Like the Bereans of Acts 17, believers should be known as those who are "examining the Scriptures" to see what is true and what is false. So, what are the essential issues that Christians should think about when choosing a church, buying a book, or tuning in to Christian radio? This chapter addresses these questions—focusing on the non-negotiables that every believer should consider when evaluating a Christian ministry, philosophy, or program.

On July 1, 1750, after twenty-three years of pastoral ministry, America's foremost theologian resigned from his church. But, unlike what we might expect today, it was not because of some moral issue in his own life. And it wasn't due to poor preaching or an unpleasant personality. It didn't even involve money issues or a building project. Instead, his reasons were doctrinal. At age forty-seven, with eight children at home, Jonathan Edwards knew that leaving his life's work would not be easy. But he also knew that the alternative, to actively endorse wrong doctrine, was unacceptable. His convictions left him with no choice.

The seeds of the controversy had actually been planted some seventy years earlier. In 1677, Solomon Stoddard (Edwards's grandfather) introduced the Halfway Covenant to his congregation in Northampton, Massachusetts. According to this covenant, well-behaved church attenders could participate in the Lord's Supper even if they had never made an outward profession of faith. In other words, they could enjoy Communion even if they were not saved.

In 1727 Edwards agreed to co-pastor the Northampton church with his grandfather. He became the sole pastor two years later, when Stoddard died. As the years passed, Edwards grew increasingly concerned about the Halfway Covenant, especially as the number of unsaved church attenders grew larger than the number of true believers.

By 1748 Edwards knew that he could no longer allow unsaved church attenders to continue participating in what Scripture clearly reserves for believers. So in early 1750 he decided to hold open lectures during the week to discuss the Lord's Supper. As one might expect, the fallout from these lectures came swiftly.

On June 2, 1750, Edwards's church council voted to terminate his pastorship at the Northampton church. The council's decision was confirmed by a congregational vote, which approved of Edwards's dismissal by a vote of 230-23. After nearly a quarter-century of service, this faithful minister was officially dismissed on June 22, 1750; he gave his "Farewell Sermon" on July 1.

But why did Edwards make such a big deal out of the Halfway Covenant issue? Surely, he could have left this issue alone and enjoyed many more years at his beloved church. But this would have been nothing more than compromise. Edwards realized that the gospel was at stake and that the eternity of his people was on the line. He could not continue confusing the unsaved, making them feel comfortable and safe though they had never personally embraced Christ. He knew they needed to repent, and that is why he took a stand. He saw it as a hill to die on.

KNOWING WHAT HILLS TO DIE ON

In reflecting on Edwards's actions, I believe at least three basic doctrines motivated him to take a stand for his convictions. The first was his appreciation for the doctrine of the Bible. Put simply, Edwards had a high view of God's Word. He knew Scripture teaches that Communion is for believers only (specifically in 1 Cor 11). For him to do nothing, allowing the Halfway Covenant to continue, would have been a clear violation of God's written standard.

Second, Edwards had a high view of God's Person. In his estimation, to obey God was far more important than to obey man (cf. Acts 5:29). He understood that his allegiance to the Sovereign of the universe took priority over his ministry status in Northampton. As a result, his choice to please God, even if it displeased his neighbors, was not really that difficult to make.

Third, Edwards had a high view of God's salvation and the gospel. When he appeased the consciences of the unsaved attenders in his congregation, he recognized that he was obscuring their view of the gospel. He realized how unacceptable it was to overlook their lack of faith and repentance, choosing instead to commend them for their outwardly good behavior. Ultimately he loved the purity of the gospel more than his position at the church.

It is these three elements—a high view of God's Word, a high view of God Himself, and a high view of the gospel—that, I believe, comprise the biblical framework for determining what hills Christians should die on. Because these three theological categories are of primary importance, believers should be careful to evaluate every ministry and every message they encounter through this doctrinal grid. Where you go to church, what books you buy, how you respond to the sermons you hear, and with whom you associate and minister—each of these should be primarily evaluated on this basis. With that in mind, let's consider each of these three theological categories.

A HIGH VIEW OF GOD'S WORD

If we are to develop biblical discernment, we must begin with a high view of the Scriptures. After all, they alone constitute God's written revelation to man. Without them, we would know nothing about God's specific desires for us or about His plan of salvation. We would be unable to please Him, to know Him, or to follow Him—being destined instead to spiritual ignorance, decay, and death. Yet God, in His mercy, revealed Himself to us in this one book we call the Bible.

For this reason, God's Word to the Christian should be like bread to the hungry man (cf. Matt 4:4) or like water to the thirsty deer (cf. Ps 42:1). By keeping its commands, we keep ourselves pure (cf. Ps 119:9). By following its guidance, we have a light for our paths (cf. Ps 119:105). By meditating on it, we find blessing and joy (cf. Ps 1:1-2). And by wrestling with it, we find our own lives being changed and sanctified (cf. Heb 4:12). It is our perfect guide and our ultimate authority (cf. Ps 19:7-11)—because it is the very Word of God. Listen to how one writer describes this magnificent book:

> This book contains: the mind of God, the state of man, the way of salvation, the doom of sinners, and the happiness of believers.
>
> Its doctrine is holy, its precepts are binding, its histories are true, and its decisions are immutable. Read it to be wise, believe it to be saved, and practice it to be holy.
>
> It contains light to direct you, food to support you, and comfort to cheer you. It is the traveler's map, the pilgrim's staff, the pilot's compass, the soldier's sword, and the Christian's charter. Here heaven is open, and the gates of hell are disclosed.
>
> Christ is the grand subject, our good its design, and the glory of God its end. It should fill the memory, rule the heart, and guide the feet.

Read it slowly, frequently, and prayerfully. It is a mine of wealth, health to the soul, and a river of pleasure. It is given to you here in this life, will be opened at the judgment, and is established forever.

It involves the highest responsibility, will reward the greatest labor, and condemn all who trifle with its contents.[1]

It's no wonder the Bereans were commended when they compared what Paul was teaching to what the Scriptures said (Acts 17:11). Churches, sermons, books, and articles may claim to be Christian. But if they undermine or contradict God's Word in any way, you can be certain they don't meet God's approval. Sometimes these errors take away from what God has taught (like the Jesus Seminar, which denies the historical authenticity of large portions of the Gospels). Other times they try to add to what God has taught (for example, cult groups who place the teachings of their leaders on the same level as the Bible). But in either case, the Scripture itself responds with strong condemnation. Consider Christ's final warning in the book of Revelation (the book that completed the New Testament canon):

> *I warn everyone who hears the words of the prophecy of this book: if anyone adds to them, God will add to him the plagues described in this book, and if anyone takes away from the words of the book of this prophecy, God will take away his share in the tree of life and in the holy city, which are described in this book. (22:18-19)*

Without question, maintaining a high view of Scripture is a hill that every Christian should die on. If God's Word is undermined, such that God Himself is no longer given the final say, then the door is opened to all kinds of error. A high view of Scripture is absolutely indispensable to the discerning Christian, and this high view must uphold at least three elements.

The authenticity of Scripture. First, a proper view of Scripture necessitates a full understanding and acknowledgment of the Bible's authenticity—namely, that the Bible is indeed the inspired Word of God. Scripture, of course, makes this claim about itself in numerous places (cf. 1 Thess 2:13; 2 Pet 1:20-21; 1 John 5:10). In fact, in the Old Testament alone, the text claims to represent the very words of God over 3,800 times. It's no wonder that, when we come to the New Testament, the apostle Paul can confidently say, "All Scripture is breathed out by God and profitable for teaching, for reproof, for correction, and for training in righteousness, that the man of God may be competent, equipped for every good work" (2 Tim 3:16-17).

Yet, despite the clear self-claims of Scripture, contemporary Christianity is fraught with attacks on the inspiration and authenticity of the Bible. Some claim that only certain parts of the Bible are inspired. Others suggest that "inspiration" doesn't actually refer to divine authorship, but rather to human intellectual achievement (similar to the emotional "inspiration" that undergirds a passionate love song). But these are really only futile attempts to deny that God Himself stands behind every word of both the Old and New Testaments (cf. Matt 5:18; 24:35). And it is at this foundational point that many so-called Christians condemn themselves to lives of perpetual confusion—doomed to wallow in the mire of man-made musings, simply because they have rejected the true source of divine wisdom. True wisdom begins with the Word of the Lord: "For the LORD gives wisdom; from his mouth come knowledge and understanding" (Prov 2:6). So unless we acknowledge that the Bible is indeed His Word, we forfeit all possibility of learning discernment.

The accuracy of Scripture. Second, a high view of Scripture must accept the accuracy and inerrancy of the Bible. After all, if the Bible is God's inspired Word in every part (meaning that He is the author), then it must also be truthful in every part (including passages regarding science and history) because He is a God of truth (cf. Titus 1:2; Heb 6:17-18). Thus, the Scriptures can be wholly trusted because they come from a God who can be wholly trusted.

This means that Genesis should be believed when it states that the world was created in seven days. It means that Adam should be accepted as a real human being, that the Flood was a global event, that Sodom and Gomorrah were literally destroyed by fire from heaven, and that Jonah was, in fact, in the belly of a fish for three days. Even Christ and the apostles reflect this same attitude toward the Old Testament when they refer to Adam (Rom 5:14), Noah (Matt 24:37-38), the inhabitants of Sodom and Gomorrah (Matt 10:15), and Jonah (Matt 12:40) as historical figures. It is not enough to accept the Scriptures as true in matters of faith and practice but deny its truthfulness in matters of history and science. If the God of truth has spoken (no matter the subject), then He has spoken truthfully.

Too often Christians accept false teachings because they trust the latest scientific or literary theories over the very Word of God. In doing so, believers relinquish their ability to discern truth from error. Why? The reason is simple: It's because they have let go of the truth, without which they have no standard for deciphering what's wrong from what's right.

The authority of Scripture. A high view of Scripture also demands submission to its absolute authority. Because the Bible comes from God Himself, and because it reflects His perfect truthfulness, it also bears His authority as the final say in our thoughts, our words, and our actions. Because we submit to Him, we likewise submit to His Word, through the power of His Spirit (John 14:15).

Without question, God should be our ultimate authority in discerning truth from error. That's why He gave us His Word—so we can know what He thinks about any given topic and thereby know the truth (cf. John 17:17). Second Peter 1:2-3 indicates that the knowledge He's given us in the Scripture includes everything we need for life and godliness. This means that we don't have to supplement the Bible with human philosophy (like the Christian psychologist does). Nor do we need business principles to learn about successful church growth (like market-driven ministries would like us to think). God has given us His authoritative word on all of those matters—and it comes complete with everything we need to live the Christian life successfully.

So what does all this mean for those who desire discernment? It means that Christians should stop endorsing or entertaining any teaching that undermines, redefines, or rejects the clear teaching of Scripture. And it also means that the Bible is the first place you should go if you want to receive a heart of wisdom (Prov 1:1-7).

A HIGH VIEW OF GOD

Another essential component in developing a framework for biblical discernment is a high view of God Himself. Of course, in order for this view to be correct, it must flow from the revelation He has given us about Himself. We must rely on His Word to inform our understanding of who He is.

Throughout church history, the doctrine of God (along with the doctrines of Christ and of the Holy Spirit) have faced many attacks. Questions about the Trinity, divine attributes, Christ's deity, and the personhood of the Holy Spirit have each been the topic of at least one church council. More recently, questions about God's sovereignty and the gifts of the Holy Spirit have sparked controversy. But in each of these areas, as believers make their way through the maze of theological rhetoric, only a biblically-informed view of God will allow them to think rightly.

A biblical view of the Sovereign. God's greatness quickly emerges from the pages of Scripture as one of His primary characteristics. It is seen in the first verse of the Bible—His creative power and His eternal preexistence. It continues in Genesis 3 with His judgment on the human race, a judgment that culminates in Genesis 6—8 with the Flood. At Sinai the mountain trembles because God is there. Even Moses, after requesting to see the Lord, is only given a sheltered glance—and he barely survives the experience.

In Psalm 115:3 we are told that "Our God is in the heavens; he does all that he pleases." In Isaiah 40:18 the Lord asks rhetorically, "To whom then will you liken God?" But the answer to this question leaves Job dumbfounded (Job 40:4-5), and the thought of God's transcendence leads Nebuchadnezzar to decree:

Blessed be the God of Shadrach, Meshach, and Abednego, who has sent his angel and delivered his servants, who trusted in him, and set aside the king's command, and yielded up their bodies rather than serve and worship any god except their own God. Therefore I make a decree: Any people, nation, or language that speaks anything against the God of Shadrach, Meshach, and Abednego shall be torn limb from limb, and their houses laid in ruins, for there is no other god who is able to rescue in this way. (Dan 3:28-29)

Yet despite God's majestic self-portrait, many Christians today are trying to minimize His greatness and His glory. In some circles, His sovereign power is denied (as with Openness Theology). In other circles it seems Satan and demons are feared more than God Himself (as in some charismatic contexts). But the Lord whom we serve is not like us. He made the sun, moon, and stars (Ps 8:3). We are not at liberty to mold Him into our image.

In discerning truth from error, we must ask ourselves, "Does a particular teaching accurately depict the God of the Bible? Does it correctly represent His character, essence, and being?" Refuse to accept any teaching where the answer is other than "yes."

A biblical view of the Savior. God's greatness and majesty is not only seen in His sovereign power, but also in His mercy and grace. In fact, it was because of the Father's great love for us that He sent His Son to die for our sins (cf. John 3:16).

As God in human flesh (cf. John 1:1, 14; Titus 2:13; Heb 1:8; 1 John 5:20), Jesus Christ lived a perfect life before sacrificing Himself on the cross. As the spotless lamb (1 Pet 1:19) and once-for-all sacrifice (Heb 10:12), He not only paid the price for our sins but also clothes us in His righteousness (2 Cor 5:21). As the risen Lord (1 Cor 15:1-8), He sits enthroned at the right hand of God the Father (Acts 7:56), waiting for the day when He will return to earth to set up His kingdom (2 Thess 1:7-10; Rev 20:1-6). In the meantime, all who trust Him as their Savior and choose to follow Him as Lord will be saved (Rom 10:9-10).

Despite the biblical evidence, false teachers continually stir up confusion about who Jesus Christ really is. Many deny his deity outright (such as the Jehovah's Witnesses who deny the Trinity altogether). Others are more subtle, agreeing that Christians must accept Jesus as Savior but not necessarily as Lord. Some even suggest that the resurrection was spurious or that the true Christ has been misrepresented by the church. But when compared to the clear testimony of Scripture, all such accusations fall flat. And that's why a biblical view of the Savior is so important for those who seek discernment.

A biblical view of the Spirit. A proper view of God the Father and God the Son would not be complete if it did not include a right view of God the Holy Spirit. Before Jesus left, He promised that He would send a Helper, the Holy Spirit, to guide Christians throughout the church age (John 14:26)—a promise that was fulfilled on the Day of Pentecost (Acts 2:2-8).

The Bible clearly distinguishes the Spirit as a separate Person (John 14:26; Rom 8:11, 16, 26; 1 John 5:7) who is equal with the Father and the Son (Matt 28:19; 2 Cor 3:16-18; 13:14; Eph 4:4-6). His ministry is one of teaching (John 14:26; Luke 12:12), interceding (Rom 8:26), leading (Matt 4:1), giving life (John 6:63), filling (Eph 5:18), and sanctifying (Gal 5:16-22). As believers study God's Word, the Spirit aids us in the process (John 14:26; 16:13; 1 Cor 2:14). In fact, Ephesians 6:17 tells us that "the sword of the Spirit," the weapon He uses to help us fend off deception, is the Word of God. It's no wonder, then, that to be filled with the Spirit (Eph 5:18) is parallel to "let[ting] the word of Christ dwell in you richly" (Col 3:16).

Confusion about the doctrine of the Holy Spirit is almost as old as the church itself. In fact, in Acts 8 a man named Simon incorrectly assumed that He could buy the Holy Spirit's power with money. Over the centuries, various cult groups—such as the Jehovah's Witnesses—have simply denied the Spirit's personhood or deity, choosing instead to see Him as an impersonal force. And, during the last hundred years especially, debate has raged over how spiritual gifts should operate in the church. Needless to say, the unbiblical practices of some charismatic groups (such as slaying in the Spirit, laughing in the Spirit, barking in the Spirit, and so on) have only increased the confusion.

But the discerning Christian is spiritually unaffected by heretical trends like these. He is like a tree, firmly planted (cf. Ps 1:3) because His view of God (including the Father, the Son, and the Spirit) is firmly founded in the truths of Scripture. By letting God's self-portrait inform his own thinking, the discerning Christian compares what he hears with what he knows to be correct. In other words, he refuses to replace a high view of God (one that is biblically accurate) with any type of cheap substitute.

A HIGH VIEW OF THE GOSPEL

Biblical discernment demands a third theological component—namely, a right understanding of the gospel. Building on the previous two categories, the gospel answers the question for us, "What must one do to be saved?" This, in fact, is the most important question human beings can ask, for our answer to that question determines both our present choices and our eternal destinies.

Sadly, many Christians downplay key aspects of the gospel message (such as the lordship of Christ discussed above). As a result, false professions of faith are commonplace in the contemporary church, where belief is redefined as mere assent, and repentance is missed altogether. But discerning Christians are not impressed with watered-down gospel presentations, nor are they fooled by the false promises of prosperity preachers. Instead they have a clear grasp of the gospel, always being ready to give an account for the hope that is in them (cf. 1 Pet 3:15).

A right view of sin. The good news of Scripture actually begins with bad news—namely, that all men are sinners before a holy God (Rom 3:23), unable to save themselves (Isa 64:6) and therefore worthy of His condemnation (Rom 6:23). Because Adam and Eve broke God's law (Gen 3:6-7), and because all of their descendants (with the exception of Jesus Christ) have also broken His law (cf. Jas 2:10), human beings deserve to be punished. As a perfect

Judge, God's judgment for sin is death—both physical (Gen 3:3) and spiritual (Rom 5:12-19). Scripture teaches that men and women are not only sinners through their actions (1 John 1:8, 10), but also because they inherited a sin nature from Adam and Eve (cf. Ps 51:5; Rom 5:12-19).

In light of Scripture's unmistakable emphasis on sin, it's disheartening to watch some contemporary Christians purposely deemphasize the subject. Rather than addressing man's true need (to be forgiven), too many modern evangelists focus on the felt needs of their audience. In the end, God is misrepresented as a loving grandfather rather than a holy Judge, and the listeners are given false expectations about the wonderful life Jesus has planned for them. Any new "converts" spend the rest of their Christian lives trying to meet their own felt needs and never really dealing with the sin in their lives—choosing instead to ignore it or to redefine it as "honest mistakes" or "unhealed wounds." In contrast, the discerning Christian is all-too-familiar with his own sinfulness, having cried out for God's mercy and daily battling the flesh (cf. Rom 7:13—8:4).

A right view of self. If you have a biblical view of your sin, you will naturally have a right view of yourself. Like Isaiah who cried out, "Woe is me!" (Isa 6:4) or the publican who pleaded, "God, be merciful to me, a sinner!" (Luke 18:13), those who recognize their sinfulness before a holy God immediately realize how wretched and unimportant they really are. With this in mind, the apostle Paul commands his readers not to think more highly of themselves than they ought to think (Rom 12:3). Instead, following the example of Christ, they should regard others with "humility," putting the wishes of their neighbor above their own (Phil 2:3-4). Past successes and achievements are deemed as worthless compared to knowing and serving the Savior (Phil 3:7-8).

For the Christian, self-esteem is replaced with self-denial. After all, we "have been crucified with Christ," meaning that we no longer live, but rather Christ lives in us (Gal 2:20). The Lord Himself instructs us along these lines, saying: "If anyone would come after me, let him deny himself and take up his cross and follow me. For whoever would save his life will lose it, but whoever loses his life for my sake and the gospel's will save it" (Mark 8:34-35). Clearly, then, this attitude of self-denial is intimately tied to the gospel, since we can do nothing, in and of ourselves, to earn salvation (Eph 2:8-9). In embracing Christ's work on our behalf, we abandon any form of self-sufficiency, choosing instead to thank God that He has chosen us—the weak, the foolish, and the unimportant (1 Cor 1:26-29).

In an age where self-esteem and self-promotion are prevalent, it's not surprising to find many in the church who have embraced their own self-worth. This problem is only compounded by the fact that sin is deemphasized, leading many pew-sitters to overestimate their own inherent goodness. God's holiness, of course, is also overlooked, resulting in Christians who have a high view of themselves and a low view of their Creator. The messages they hear and the books they read are therefore evaluated by their own man-made standards—in terms of felt needs and innovative programs. Because of their diminished reverence for God, they do not look to Him for His approval. And as a result they fail to cultivate true discernment in their lives.

A right view of salvation. Having underestimated sin and having overestimated themselves, these same Christians fail to properly understand salvation. In some cases they begin to view salvation as nothing more than heavenly fire insurance (a "Get Out of Hell Free" card)—as though God is obligated to save them without any repentance on their part. Others misunderstand grace, including cults like Roman Catholicism, where works-righteousness is added to God's free gift. Key concepts, such as justification and imputation (Christ takes our sin, and we take His righteousness) are sometimes misunderstood or redefined (as with the New Perspective on Paul). There are even some, such as Seventh-Day Adventists, who claim Christ's atonement on the cross was not His final work of atonement—despite verses such as Hebrews 7:27 and 1 Peter 3:18.

So what is the biblical plan of salvation from sin? The apostle Paul succinctly answers this question in Romans 10:9-10 when he says, "if you confess with your mouth that Jesus is Lord and believe in your heart that God raised him from the dead, you will be saved. For with the heart one believes and is justified, and with the mouth one confesses and is saved." And in 1 Corinthians 15:1-4 he reiterates these truths:

> Now I would remind you, brothers, of the gospel I preached to you, which you received, in which you stand, and by which you are being saved, if you hold fast to the word I preached to you—unless you believed in vain. For I delivered to you as of first importance what I also received: that Christ died for our sins in accordance with the Scriptures, that he was buried, that he was raised on the third day in accordance with the Scriptures.

Thus, the call of salvation is a call to believe in the once-for-all sacrifice of Jesus Christ on the cross, and to publicly submit ("confess") oneself to Him as Lord (thereby repenting from sin). Of course, this is a gift of grace and not of human effort or merit (Eph 2:8-10). And it also involves other theological truths—such as regeneration (John 3:3-7; Titus 3:5), election (Rom 8:28-30; Eph 1:4-11; 2 Thess 2:13), sanctification (Acts 20:32; 1 Cor 1:2, 30; 6:11; Heb 10:10, 14), and eternal security (John 5:24; 6:37-40; 10:27-30; Rom 5:9-10; 8:31-39). But the heart of the gospel is this: By dying on the cross, Jesus took the penalty for all who believe in Him. And by trusting in Him, the believer is seen as righteous (or justified) in the sight of God.

Thinking rightly about the gospel is something God takes very seriously. In fact, Scripture severely condemns those who preach another gospel as false teachers (Gal 1:8). Christians would do well, then, to arm themselves with the true gospel—one that maintains a biblical view of sin, self, and salvation. Only then will we be able to fulfill the Great Commission with which we have been tasked (Matt 28:18-20); and only then will we be able to discern the message of life from any counterfeits. False gospels cannot be tolerated because eternity is at stake.

MOUNTAINS AND MOLEHILLS

Are there other hills that Christians should die on? Possibly, depending on the circumstances and the individuals involved. Questions about end times, about the church, and about other areas of theology are certainly important. So why did we focus on the Bible, God, and the gospel? The answer is simply this: The New Testament portrays an accurate understanding of these three doctrines as absolutely essential.

For example, Peter discusses all three in the first two verses of his second epistle—an epistle that spends most of its time refuting false teaching. He begins with a right view of salvation (faith by the righteousness of Jesus Christ). He quickly moves to a right view of Jesus Christ (as "our God and Savior" and "our Lord"). And He mentions a right view of the Scriptures ("the knowledge of God"), a subject he unpacks in the rest of chapter 1. Other New Testament writers agree, responding to false gospels (Gal 1:6-7; 2 Cor 11:4), false christs (1 John 2:22; 2 John 7), and mishandled Scriptures (2 Pet 3:16) with the harshest of criticisms (Matt 24:24; 2 Pet 2:1-22; Jude 4-19). Because Christ and the apostles took a firm stand on these issues, we should be careful to do the same.

We should also take note of those issues that Scripture does not list as hills to die on. For example, preference issues such as the length of a sermon, the style of music used in corporate worship, the church's building program, and other pet grievances are not issues on which we should refuse to budge. Although we live in a day when everyone demands his or her personal rights, opinions, and choices, our testimony as Christians should be different, seeking to give preferential treatment to our brothers and sisters in Christ (Phil 2:1-4).

CONCLUSION

When it comes to developing discernment, we cannot overstate the importance of a theological grid through which every message is filtered. Without sound doctrine, you will not be able to protect your own heart from the many doctrinal errors that exist today. But by looking to the Scripture (as your ultimate authority) for a right view of God and a right view of the gospel, you can safeguard your mind—"We destroy arguments and every lofty opinion raised against the knowledge of God, and take every thought captive to obey Christ" (2 Cor 10:5).

Jonathan Edwards serves as an excellent example of how good theology allows us to discern between what is right and what is wrong. Because he knew the clear teaching of Scripture, because he revered the holiness of his Master, and because he feared the endorsement of a false gospel, he took a stand for the truth. Yes, it cost him his ministry, his paycheck, and probably a few friends. But in the end he was convinced that faithfulness to God was more important. The same is true for us today as we allow God's truth to dictate the issues we fight for and the hills we die on.

12

KEEPING THE FAITH:
A PRACTICAL PLAN FOR
PERSONAL DISCERNMENT[1]

John MacArthur

This book opened with a call for biblical discernment. In keeping with this theme, this chapter details a practical plan for cultivating personal discernment in the Christian life. The importance of personal discernment cannot be overstated because those who are unable to distinguish right from wrong will likely fall into serious error. Christians need to realize that this error comes in many forms, and it often looks good at first glance—that's why it's called deception. Yet, God has given His children all that they need to "test everything; hold fast what is good. Abstain from every form of evil" (1 Thess 5:21-22). Thus we can be confident that those who learn to think biblically will be adequately equipped to "turn away from the snares of death" (Prov 14:27). By asking the question, "How can we do this?"—and looking to God's Word for the answer—this chapter will help us spot, and reject, fool's gold.

When Aben Johnson sold his Detroit-based television station in 1997, he began heavily investing in gemstones. While he had dabbled in diamonds since 1988, he now had the capital he needed to purchase the rarest stones money could buy. He spent three million dollars on a blue diamond called the Streeter Diamond that Sam Walton (the founder of Wal-Mart) had won in a poker game from a man named Streeter. Johnson spent $2.7 million for a collection of diamonds called the Russian Blues. Another seventeen million dollars was invested in the Sylvia Walton Collection—a set of diamonds that belonged to Sam Walton's daughter. In all, Johnson invested some eighty-three million dollars in the costly gems.

But what Johnson didn't realize was that these famous-named diamonds, which he thought were priceless, were actually almost worthless. In fact, they were not diamonds at all. The stones were actually cubic zirconia, blue topaz, citrine, and other inexpensive gems. To add insult to injury, Sam Walton never had a daughter named Sylvia.

When Johnson found out that his Florida-based jeweler, Jack Hasson, had bilked him, he filed suit. A year later, in 1999, the FBI arrested Hasson for fraud. In 2000 he was convicted, sentenced to forty years in prison, and ordered to pay more than seventy-eight million dollars in restitution.

Despite his legal efforts, Johnson will never be able to fully recover his eighty-three million dollars. If only he had exercised a little discernment before parting with his millions. Some simple tests of the diamonds by a gemologist or appraiser could have saved Johnson a bundle of money and trouble.

One test uses a thermal conductivity meter, another an ordinary microscope. Such tests for authenticity certainly seem worth the effort when millions of dollars are at stake. Yet, like Aben Johnson, Christians often fall for bait-and-switch ploys, and we have something infinitely more valuable than diamonds at stake—namely, God's glory.

Thankfully, by God's grace we have a standard by which to test the authenticity of any incoming religious message. That's why, even when we are bombarded with doctrinal frauds and spiritual knock-offs, we need not lose hope. God has not left us defenseless. By arming us with His Word, He has given us everything we need for "life and godliness" (2 Pet 1:3).

TRENDS, TRADITIONS, AND THE SUFFICIENCY OF SCRIPTURE

Our reliance on the Scriptures becomes more and more crucial every day, as new errors are introduced into the church and as old errors continue to resurface. On the one hand, "new and improved" programs and philosophies appeal to us with their siren calls. Whether it's new ways to evangelize or new ways to fill the auditorium, these innovative trends always seem to provide the perfect solution for the church's present needs. But these new "solutions," primarily based on secular wisdom and driven by whatever works, do not really solve anything. By suggesting that the "old and original" methods of the New Testament are no longer good enough for today, these theological trends are really just worldly philosophies in religious garb.

On the other hand, theological traditions (sometimes centuries old) also vie for our attention. Many of these traditions are good, but some of them are not. And they have been established for almost every aspect of Christian thought, from methods of church government to philosophies of Bible interpretation. Unlike their "new and improved" counterparts, these historic systems appeal to their distinguished heritage for added credibility. Nonetheless, when these theological legacies begin to replace the clear teachings of Scripture (as has happened, for example, in the Roman Catholic Church), the results are disastrous.

So how can believers discern between trends, traditions, and the truth? As we saw in chapter 1, the answer to this question begins with the Scriptures. God has given us His Word so that we can evaluate every spiritual message we receive, discriminating between what is right and what is wrong. In 2 Timothy 3:16-17, the apostle Paul said it like this:

All Scripture is breathed out by God and profitable for teaching, for reproof, for correction, and for training in righteousness, that the man of God may be competent, equipped for every good work.

Do you want to be equipped for *every* good work? Do you

want to be able to teach truth and correct error? If so, you must become a student of the Scriptures—trusting that His Word is a sufficient guide for any problem you encounter. The maze of modern religious thought is no match for the Sword of the Spirit, which is able even to "discern the thoughts and intentions of the heart" (Heb 4:12).

A PRACTICAL PLAN FOR DEVELOPING DISCERNMENT

So how can Christians, practically speaking, begin to apply biblical discernment to their daily lives? In the preceding chapters you've seen several examples of poor theology and the confusion it can cause. So how can you prepare yourself for the battle? How can you make sure that you are guarding the truth of God's Word, so that you will be able to faithfully pass it on to the next generation? I believe Scripture outlines the following plan for us to follow.

DESIRE WISDOM

Step 1 is *desire*. Proverbs 2:3-6 says, "if you call out for insight and raise your voice for understanding, if you seek it like silver and search for it as for hidden treasures, then you will understand the fear of the LORD and find the knowledge of God. For the LORD gives wisdom; from his mouth come knowledge and understanding."

If we have no desire to be discerning, we won't be discerning. If we are driven by a yearning to be happy, healthy, affluent, prosperous, comfortable, and self-satisfied, we will never be discerning people. If our feelings determine what we believe, we cannot be discerning. If we subjugate our minds to some earthly ecclesiastical authority and blindly believe what we are told, we undermine discernment. Unless we are willing to examine all things carefully, we cannot hope to have any defense against reckless faith.

The desire for discernment is a desire born out of humility. It is a humility that acknowledges our own potential for self-deception ("The heart is deceitful above all things, and desperately sick;

who can understand it?"—Jer 17:9). It is a humility that distrusts personal feelings and casts scorn on self-sufficiency ("on my own behalf I will not boast, except of my weaknesses," 2 Cor 12:5). It is a humility that turns to the Word of God as the final arbiter of all things ("examining the Scriptures daily to see if these things were so," Acts 17:11).

No one has a monopoly on truth. I certainly do not. I don't have reliable answers within myself. My heart is as susceptible to self-deception as anyone's. My feelings are as undependable as everyone else's. I am not immune to Satan's deception. That is true for all of us. Our only defense against false doctrine is to be discerning, to distrust our own emotions, to hold our own senses suspect, to examine all things, to test every truth-claim with the yardstick of Scripture, and to handle the Word of God with great care.

The desire to be discerning therefore entails a high view of Scripture linked with an enthusiasm for understanding it correctly. God requires that very attitude (2 Tim 2:15). So the heart that truly loves Him will naturally burn with a passion for discernment.

PRAY FOR DISCERNMENT

Step two is *prayer*. Prayer, of course, naturally follows desire; prayer is the expression of the heart's desire to God.

When Solomon became king after the death of David, the Lord appeared to him in a dream and said, "Ask what I shall give you" (1 Kings 3:5). Solomon could have requested anything. He could have asked for material riches, power, victory over his enemies, or whatever he liked. But Solomon asked for discernment: "Give your servant therefore an understanding mind to govern your people, that I may discern between good and evil" (v. 9). Scripture says, "It pleased the Lord that Solomon had asked this" (v. 10).

Moreover, the Lord told Solomon,

> *Because you have asked this, and have not asked for yourself long life or riches or the life of your enemies, but have asked for yourself understanding to discern what is right, behold, I now do according to your*

word. Behold, I give you a wise and discerning mind, so that none like you has been before you and none like you shall arise after you. I give you also what you have not asked, both riches and honor, so that no other king shall compare with you, all your days. And if you will walk in my ways, keeping my statutes and my commandments, as your father David walked, then I will lengthen your days. (vv. 11-14)

Notice that God commended Solomon because his request was completely *unselfish*: "because you have asked this, and have not asked for yourself . . ." Selfishness is incompatible with true discernment. People who desire to be discerning must be willing to step outside themselves.

Modern evangelicalism, enamored with psychology and self-esteem, has produced a generation of believers so self-absorbed that they *cannot* be discerning. People aren't even interested in discernment. All their interest in spiritual things is focused on self. They are interested only in getting their own felt needs met.

Solomon did not do that. Although he had an opportunity to ask for long life, personal prosperity, health and wealth, he bypassed all of that and asked for discernment instead. Therefore God also gave him riches, honor, and long life for as long as he walked in the ways of the Lord.

James 1:5 promises that God will grant the prayer for discernment generously: "If any of you lacks wisdom, let him ask God, who gives generously to all without reproach, and it will be given him."

OBEY THE TRUTH

Someone will point out that with all his abundance of wisdom, Solomon was nevertheless a dismal failure at the end of his life (1 Kings 11:4-11). "His heart was not wholly true to the LORD his God, as was the heart of David his father" (v. 4). Scripture records this sad assessment of the wisest man who ever lived:

Now King Solomon loved many foreign women, along with the daughter of Pharaoh: Moabite, Ammonite, Edomite, Sidonian, and

Hittite women, from the nations concerning which the LORD had said
to the people of Israel, "You shall not enter into marriage with them,
neither shall they with you, for surely they will turn away your heart
after their gods." Solomon clung to these in love. He had 700 wives,
princesses, and 300 concubines. And his wives turned away his heart.
For when Solomon was old his wives turned away his heart after other
gods, and his heart was not wholly true to the LORD his God, as was
the heart of David his father. For Solomon went after Ashtoreth the
goddess of the Sidonians, and after Milcom the abomination of the
Ammonites. So Solomon did what was evil in the sight of the LORD
and did not wholly follow the LORD, as David his father had done.
Then Solomon built a high place for Chemosh the abomination of
Moab, and for Molech the abomination of the Ammonites, on the
mountain east of Jerusalem. And so he did for all his foreign wives,
who made offerings and sacrificed to their gods. And the LORD was
angry with Solomon, because his heart had turned away from the
LORD. (vv. 1-9)

But Solomon did not suddenly fail at the end of his life. The
seeds of his demise were sown at the very beginning. First Kings 3,
the same chapter that records Solomon's request for discernment,
also reveals that Solomon "made a marriage alliance with Pharaoh
king of Egypt" (v. 1). Verse 3 tells us, "Solomon loved the LORD,
walking in the statutes of David his father, only he sacrificed and
made offerings at the high places."

From the very beginning his obedience was deficient. Surely
with all his wisdom he knew better, but he tolerated compromise and
idolatry among the people of God (v. 2)—and even participated in
some of the idolatry himself!

Discernment is not enough apart from *obedience*. What good is it
to know the truth if we fail to act accordingly? That is why James
wrote, "be doers of the word, and not hearers only, deceiving yourselves" (Jas 1:22). Failure to obey is self-delusion; it is not true discernment, no matter how much intellectual knowledge we may
possess. Solomon is biblical proof that even true discernment can give
way to a destructive self-delusion. Disobedience inevitably under-

mines discernment. The only way to guard against that is to be doers of the Word and not hearers only.

FOLLOW DISCERNING LEADERS

Fourth in our series of steps toward biblical discernment is this: *Emulate those who demonstrate good discernment.* Do not follow the leadership of people who are themselves "tossed to and fro by the waves and carried about by every wind of doctrine" (Eph 4:14). Find and follow leaders who display an ability to discern, to analyze and refute error, to teach the Scriptures clearly and accurately. Read from authors who prove themselves careful handlers of divine truth. Listen to preachers who rightly divide the Word of Truth. Expose yourself to the teaching of people who think critically, analytically, and carefully. Learn from people who understand where error has attacked the church historically. Place yourself under the tutelage of those who serve as watchmen of the church.

I do this myself. There are certain authors who have demonstrated skill in handling the Word and whose judgment I have come to trust. When I encounter a difficult issue—whether it is a theological problem, an area of controversy, a new teaching I have never heard before, or whatever—I turn to these authors first to see what they have to say. I wouldn't seek help from an unreliable source or a marginal theologian. I want to know what those who are skilled in exposing error and are gifted in presenting truth have to say.

There have been outstanding men of discernment in virtually every era of church history. Their writings remain invaluable resources for anyone who wishes to cultivate discernment. Martyn Lloyd-Jones and J. Gresham Machen are just two of many in the past century who distinguished themselves in the battle for truth. Charles Spurgeon, Charles Hodge, and scores of other writers from the nineteenth century left a rich legacy of written material to help us discern between truth and error. In the century before that, Thomas Boston, Jonathan Edwards, and George Whitefield battled for truth, as did many others like them. The preceding era was the Puritan age—the sixteenth and seventeenth centuries, which gave us what is undoubtedly the richest catalog of resources for discernment. Before that, the Reformers fought valiantly for the truth of God's Word against the traditions of men. Virtually every era before the Reformation also had godly men of discernment who stood against error and defended the truth of God's Word. Augustine, for example, preceded John Calvin by more than a thousand years, but he fought exactly the same theological battles and proclaimed precisely the same doctrines. Calvin and the Reformers drew heavily on Augustine's writings as they framed their own arguments against error. In A.D. 325 a contemporary of Augustine, Athanasius, took a decisive stand against Arianism, the same error that is perpetuated by modern-day Jehovah's Witnesses. His writings stand today as the definitive response to that error.

Much of the written legacy these spiritual giants left is still available today. We can all learn from these men of discernment—and we would do well to emulate the clarity with which they spoke the truth against error.

Those who can expose and answer the errors of false teachers are set in the body of Christ to assist us all to think critically and clearly. Learn from them.

DEPEND ON THE HOLY SPIRIT

As important as human examples are, however, the Spirit of God is ultimately the true Discerner. It is His role to lead us into all truth (John 16:13). First Corinthians 2:11 says, "no one comprehends the thoughts of God except the Spirit of God." Paul goes on to write,

> *We have received . . . the Spirit who is from God, that we might understand the things freely given us by God. And we impart this in words not taught by human wisdom but taught by the Spirit, interpreting spiritual truths to those who are spiritual. The natural person does not accept the things of the Spirit of God, for they are folly to him, and he is not able to understand them because they are spiritually discerned.*

> *The spiritual person judges all things, but is himself to be judged by no one. (vv. 12-15)*

So discernment ultimately depends on the Holy Spirit. As we are filled with and controlled by the Spirit of God, He makes us discerning.

STUDY THE SCRIPTURES

Finally, we return to the point we have touched on repeatedly. It cannot be overemphasized: *True discernment requires diligent study of the Scriptures*. None of the other steps is sufficient apart from this. No one can be truly discerning apart from mastery of the Word of God. All the desire in the world cannot make you discerning if you don't study Scripture. Prayer for discernment is not enough. Obedience alone will not suffice. Good role models won't do it either. Even the Holy Spirit will not give you discernment apart from His Word. If you really want to be discerning, you must diligently study the Word of God.

God's Word is where you will learn the principles for discernment. It is there you will learn the truth. Only there can you follow the path of maturity.

Discernment flourishes only in an environment of faithful Bible study and teaching. Note that in Acts 20, when Paul was leaving the Ephesian elders, he warned them about the deadly influences that would threaten them in his absence (vv. 28-31). He urged them to be on guard, on the alert (vv. 28, 31). How? What safeguard could he leave to help protect them from Satan's onslaughts? Only the Word of God: "And now I commend you to God and to the word of his grace, which is able to build you up and to give you the inheritance among all those who are sanctified" (v. 32).

Let's look once more, closely, at 2 Timothy 2:15: "Do your best to present yourself to God as one approved, a worker who has no need to be ashamed, rightly handling the word of truth." Notice what this mandate to Timothy implies. First, it suggests that the discerning person must be able to distinguish between the Word of Truth and the "irreverent babble" mentioned in verse 16. That may seem rather obvious, but it cannot be taken for granted. The task of separating God's Word from human foolishness actually poses a formidable challenge for many today. One look at some of the nonsense that proliferates in churches and Christian media will confirm that this is so. Or note the burgeoning stacks of "Christian" books touting weird views. We must shun such folly and devote ourselves to the Word of God. We have to be able to distinguish between the truth and error.

How? "Do your best" (NASB, "Be diligent"). Being diligent pictures a worker giving maximum effort in his or her work. It describes someone driven by a commitment to excellence. "Be diligent to present yourself approved to God" (NASB). The Greek phrase literally speaks of standing alongside God as a co-laborer worthy of identifying with Him.

Furthermore, Paul says this approved workman "has no need to be ashamed." The word "ashamed" is very important to Paul's whole point. Any sloppy workman *should* be ashamed of low-quality work. But a servant of the Lord, handling the Word of Truth carelessly, has infinitely more to be ashamed of.

What Paul suggests in this passage is that we will be ashamed before God Himself if we fail to handle the Word of Truth with discernment. If we can't distinguish the truth from worldly and empty chatter, if we can't identify and refute false teachers, or if we can't handle God's truth with skill and understanding, we *ought* to be ashamed.

And if we are to divide the Word of Truth rightly, then we must be very diligent about studying it. There is no shortcut. Only as we master the Word of God are we made "competent, equipped for every good work" (3:17). That is the essence of discernment.

KEEP GROWING

Put simply, spiritual maturity is the process of learning to discern. In fact, the path to real discernment is the path to spiritual growth—and vice versa. Growth in grace is a continuous process throughout this earthly life. No Christian ever reaches complete maturity this side of heaven. "Now we see in a mirror dimly, but then face to face. Now I know in part; then I shall know fully, even as I have been fully known" (1 Cor 13:12). We must continually "grow in the grace and knowledge of our Lord and Savior Jesus Christ" (2 Pet 3:18). We should hunger "for the pure spiritual milk, that by it [we] may grow" (1 Pet 2:2).

As we mature, our senses are exercised to discern good and evil (Heb 5:14). As we cease to be children, we gain stability (Eph 4:14-15). Mature people *are* discerning people.

We know this from the natural world. The bulk of every parent's responsibility is training children to be discerning. We continually do it, even when our kids become teenagers. We help them think through issues, understand what is wise and unwise, and prompt them to make the right choices. We help them discern. In fact, the goal of parenting is to raise a discerning child. It doesn't happen automatically, and it doesn't occur without diligent, lifelong instruction.

The same is true spiritually. You don't pray for discernment and suddenly wake up with abundant wisdom. It is a process of growth.

Stay on the path of maturity. Sometimes it involves suffering and trials (Jas 1:2-4; 1 Pet 5:10). Often it necessitates divine chastening (Heb 12:11). Always it requires personal discipline (1 Tim 4:7-8). But the rewards are rich:

> *Blessed is the one who finds wisdom, and the one who gets under-standing, for the gain from her is better than gain from silver and her profit better than gold. She is more precious than jewels, and nothing you desire can compare with her. Long life is in her right hand; in her left hand are riches and honor. Her ways are ways of pleasantness, and all her paths are peace. She is a tree of life to those who lay hold of her; those who hold her fast are called blessed. . . . My son, do not lose sight of these—keep sound wisdom and discretion, and they will be life for your soul and adornment for your neck. Then you will walk on your way securely, and your foot will not stumble. (Prov 3:13-18, 21-23)*

And these riches, unlike diamonds, will retain their value and brilliance for all eternity. The alternative is a life of theological confusion, where spiritual treasures are confused with spiritual fakes.

Whoever is wise, let him understand these things; whoever is discerning, let him know them; for the ways of the LORD are right, and the upright walk in them, but transgressors stumble in them. (Hos 14:9)

NOTEƒ

Chapter 1

1. This chapter was adapted from Chapter 3 of *Reckless Faith* (Wheaton, IL: Crossway Books, 1994).
2. Jay E. Adams, *A Call to Discernment* (Eugene, OR: Harvest House, 1987), 46.
3. Ibid., 75.

Chapter 3

1. Rick Warren, *The Purpose-Driven Life* (Grand Rapids, MI: Zondervan, 2002). "Purpose-Driven" is a registered trademark.
2. William Lobdell, "Pastor with a Purpose," *The Seattle Times* (September 29, 2003): A3.
3. Warren does discuss some of these issues later in the book. However, it is surprising that he does not include them here (in Day 7), since this is the book's primary gospel presentation.
4. This "deeper-life" emphasis seems to be outlined in Chapter 10 where Warren says, "The Bible is crystal clear about how you benefit when you *fully* surrender your life to God" (p. 82, emphasis added).
5. Bob DeWaay, "The Gospel: A Method or a Message?" *Critical Issues Commentary* (January/February 2004); www.twincityfellowship.com/cic/articles/issue80.htm.
6. Rick Warren, "An Interview with Rick Warren," *Modern Reformation*, 13/1 (January/February 2004); www.modernreformation.org.
7. It is recognized that this distinction (between doctrine and duty in Paul's epistles) is somewhat artificial. In this case, however, it seems an appropriate description of a Pauline priority structure—where right living is a result of right theology.
8. DeWaay, "A Method or a Message?"
9. "Purpose-Driven Life," Internet Discussion Forum (June 10, 2004); www.livejournal.com/community/christianleft/51855.html.
10. Although they are outside of the scope of this review, more complete evaluations of *The Purpose-Driven Church*, as well as the seeker-sensitive movement, are avail-

able for those who want to learn more. Our reason for briefly mentioning them here is simply as a warning. The present author has written two related articles: "A Review of *The Purpose-Driven Church*," *Pulpit* (September/October 2003) and "The Gospel According to Hybels and Warren," *Pulpit* (November/December 2003). They are both available online at www.shepherdsfellowship.org.

Chapter 4

1. N. T. Wright, *What Saint Paul Really Said* (Grand Rapids, MI: Eerdmans, 1997).
2. I'll leave it to others to answer the New Perspective on historical grounds. D. A. Carson has made a good start on answering the claim that Protestant interpreters have historically misrepresented first-century Judaism. He is editing a two-volume academic work titled *Justification and Variegated Nomism*. The first volume, subtitled "The Complexities of Second Temple Judaism," is already available, answering the historical argument about the nature of Judaism in Paul's day. A second volume, subtitled "The Paradoxes of Paul," will deal with the exegetical issues raised by the New Perspective.
3. Sydney D. Dyer, "Tom Wright's Ecumenical Teaching," *Katekomen* (14/1). Published online at www.banneroftruth.org/pages/articles/article_detail.php?195.
4. Ibid.

Chapter 5

1. John Eldredge, *Wild at Heart* (Nashville: Thomas Nelson, 2001).
2. Jim Rosscup, "Review of *Wild at Heart*," *Pulpit* (September/October 2003).

Chapter 6

1. *Revolve: The Complete New Testament* (Nashville: Transit Books, Thomas Nelson, 2003).
2. Ellen Leventry, "Extreme Makeover: A Teen Take on the New Testament"; www.beliefnet.com/story/131/story_13171.html.
3. Agnieszka Tennant, "Ten Things You Should Know About the New Girls' Biblezine," (September 16, 2003); www.christianitytoday.com/ct/2003/137/21.0.html.
4. Wolf Blitzer, "Book Publisher: Amazing Response to Bible Magazine," Interview Transcript, (September 2, 2003); www.cnn.com/2003/SHOWBIZ/books/09/01/cnna.etue/index.html.
5. Tennant, "Ten Things."
6. David Roach, "*Revolve* New Testament Trivializes Gospel Message, Moore Says on MSNBC" (September 16, 2003); www.religionnewsblog.com/news.php?p=4444&c=1.
7. Ibid.

8. Os Guinness, *Prophetic Untimeliness* (Grand Rapids, MI: Baker Books, 2003), 15.
9. Kate Etue as cited in a Thomas Nelson Press Release issued in Summer 2003. The release was titled "Eye Candy for Bittersweet Times"; located at www.bookpros.com/Clients/Revolve/Revhome.htm.
10. Guinness, *Prophetic Untimeliness*, 54.

Chapter 7

1. John Macarthur, Joni Eareckson Tada, Robert and Bobbi Wolgemuth, Great Hymns of Our Faith: *O Worship the King* (Wheaton, IL, Crossway, 2000), *O Come, All Ye Faithful* (2001), *What Wondrous Love Is This* (2002), and *When Morning Gilds the Skies* (2002).
2. Many new hymns have been written and published since 1940, of course, but none of them has become standard church fare.
3. Robert K. Brown and Mark R. Norton, *The One Year Book of Hymns* (Wheaton, IL: Tyndale House), 1995.
4. J. C. Pollock, *Moody: A Biographical Portrait of the Pacesetter in Modern Mass Evangelism* (New York: Macmillan, 1963), 132-133.
5. Written by Julia H. Johnston (music by Daniel B. Towner).
6. I do think the style must be appropriate for the content, and for that reason I would object to some contemporary Christian music on stylistic grounds. But my first concern—and the point I'm addressing in this article—has to do with content, not style.
7. Lyrics by C. Austin Miles (1868-1946).
8. Isaac Watts, John Rippon, Augustus Toplady, and Charles Wesley are a few of the well-known hymn-writers who were first of all pastors and theologians.
9. The familiar hymn "Holy, Holy, Holy," for example, is a recitation of the divine attributes, with a particular emphasis on the doctrine of the Trinity. "Jesus, Thou Joy of Loving Hearts," an ancient but familiar hymn, is a hymn of praise to Christ filled with teaching about Christ's sufficiency.
10. In Luther's best-known hymn, "A Mighty Fortress Is Our God," each stanza builds on the previous one, and the stanzas are therefore so inextricably linked that to skip a verse is to destroy the continuity and the message of the hymn itself. It's not the type of hymn where only the first and last stanzas may be sung.
11. "How Great Thou Art" would be a prime example.
12. This concern is precisely what provoked Joni Tada, the Wolgemuths, and myself to write *O Worship The King* and the other books in the Great Hymns of Our Faith series (see footnote 1).
13. Charles Hodge, *Ephesians* (Edinburgh: Banner of Truth, 1991 reprint), 302-303.
14. Those who argue for exclusive psalmody (the view that no musical forms should be employed in the church other than metrical versions of the Old

Testament Psalms) often claim that the expression "psalms and hymns and spiritual songs" is a reference to the various categories of Davidic psalms in the Septuagint. But if the apostle Paul's intention had been to limit music in the church to the Old Testament psalms, there are many less ambiguous ways he could have made the point. On the contrary, what he is calling for here is a variety of musical forms—all employed to honor the Lord by admonishing and teaching one another with the truths of the Christian faith. Exclusive psalmody undermines that by limiting all church music to Old Testament expressions. If we follow that view and allow no lyrics in church music to go beyond the Old Testament psalms, then some of the most glorious truths at the heart of our faith—such as Christ's incarnation, His atoning death on the cross, and His resurrection—could never be explicitly featured or fully expounded upon in our music.

15. Taken from the unpublished notes of a friend who was researching church growth and worship styles in a few representative megachurches.

16. Leonard R. Payton, "Congregational Singing and the Ministry of the Word," *The Highway* (July 1998); www.gospelcom.net/thehighway/articleJuly98.html.

17. Ibid.

18. Ibid.

19. Lyrics by Walter Chalmers Smith (1824-1908). Smith was a pastor and one-time Moderator of the Free Church of Scotland.

Chapter 8

1. Cited in Iain Murray, *Pentecost Today* (Carlisle, PA: Banner of Truth, 1998), 51.

2. Jim Ehrhard, "The Dangers of the Invitation System" (Parkville, MO: Christian Communicators Worldwide, 1999), 15.

3. Ibid.

4. Ibid., 12.

5. Ibid.

6. D. Martyn Lloyd-Jones, *Preaching and Preachers* (Grand Rapids, MI: Zondervan, 1972), 274.

7. Ibid., 274-275.

8. Ibid., 277.

9. John MacArthur, sermon, "Commitments of a Powerful Leader," Audio Tape GC-56-3, 1992.

Chapter 9

1. "The Light of the World," in *The Metropolitan Tabernacle Pulpit*, Vol. 19 (London: Passmore & Alabaster, 1873), 241.

2. Ibid., 244.

Chapter 10

1. Michael Horton, *Made in America: The Shaping of Modern Evangelicalism* (Grand Rapids, MI: Baker, 1991). Cited from C. J. Mahaney, "A Passion for the Church: Why We Gather Corporately," audio sermon (Gaithersburg, MD: Sovereign Grace Ministries, 2003).

Chapter 11

1. Cited by John MacArthur, "How We Got the Bible," *The MacArthur Study Bible* (Nashville: Thomas Nelson, 1997), xviii.

Chapter 12

1. This chapter was adapted from Chapter 3 of *Reckless Faith* (Wheaton, IL: Crossway Books, 1994).

SCRIPTURE INDEX

4:7-8	206	2:11	31
6:17	161	2:23	92
6:20	29	3:15	189
		3:18	191
2 Timothy		5:10	206
1:13-14	29		
2:15	52, 108, 199, 204	*2 Peter*	
2:16	205	1:2-3	185
3:15-17	86	1:3	86, 196
3:16-17	84, 127, 184, 197	1:20-21	184
3:17	205	2	55
4:2	36, 41, 127	2:1	33
		2:1-22	193
Titus		3:16	193
1:2	184	3:18	206
1:9	23, 32		
2	95	*1 John*	
2:1-8	84	1:8, 10	190
2:2	84	2:19	29
2:10	128	2:22	193
2:13	187	5:7	188
3:5	192	5:10	184
		5:20	187
Philemon			
19	28	*2 John*	
		7	193
Hebrews			
1:8	187	*Jude*	
4:12	24, 41, 174, 182, 198	3	84
5:11-14	55	4-19	193
5:14	206	16	50
6:17-18	184		
7:25	136	*Revelation*	
7:27	191	4—5	128
10:10, 14	192	14	125
10:12	187	20:1-6	187
10:25	173	22:18	108
10:31	125	22:18-19	84, 183
12:11	206		
12:25	54		
James			
1:2-4	206		
1:5	200		
1:18	37		
1:22	201		
2:10	189		
3:1	52		
3:17	34, 55		
5:12	57		
1 Peter			
1:19	187		
1:23	37		
2:1-2	57		
2:2	206		
2:9	128		

PERSON INDEX

ЅUBJECT INDEX